FRENCH
Towards
GCSE

including

Common Entrance and Scholarship at 13+
to Independent Senior Schools

Nigel Pearce
Summer Fields, Oxford

LIBRARY OF QUALITY IN EDUCATION
Dedicated to the
Very Highest Quality Education Resource Materials

GENERAL EDITOR

K.S.Sood
B.Sc(Hons), M.Phil, ARCS

WIMBLEDON PUBLISHING COMPANY

1

FRENCH
Towards
GCSE
by Nigel Pearce

LIBRARY OF QUALITY IN EDUCATION

First Published in Great Britain in 1995

by

WIMBLEDON PUBLISHING COMPANY LIMITED
29 Hartfield Road, London SW19 3SG

ISBN 1 898855 07 2

Produced in Great Britain
Printed in Hungary
Typesetting by P.M.Graphics, London
Cover Design by Malvinder S. Soor

This book is dedicated
to the memory of

Joanna Boddington

a former pupil,
who achieved a great deal
in a very short life.

Acknowledgements

I should like to record my thanks to the following people for their help in the preparation of this book: my parents, for their invaluable moral and material support; my wife Judy, who has encouraged me throughout all the book's ups and downs; Maryse Whitcombe, Head of Modern Languages at St. Hugh's School, Woodhall Spa, Lincs., who patiently advised me on some aspects of the French texts; and Henry Phillips, Headmaster of Hordle House School, Lymington, Hants., who kindly reviewed the proofs. I should also like to thank my pupils at Summer Fields, Oxford, who (unwittingly!) did some of the exercises.

I would like to thank Hodder and Stoughton plc for permission to include an exercise based on *Le Bon Piéton*, which appears in their French course Spirale; Le Monde, for permission to reproduce a short article, and Harrap Limited, for use of a rhyme about adjectives from La Langue des Français I, by J. R. Watson

Finally, I am indebted to Nick Aldridge of Summer Fields, for generously allowing me to use his computer to work on the text.

Avant - Propos

This is primarily a reference and practice book, split into two distinct parts for these purposes, in which I have tried to address my own pupils' needs, and the short-comings in some respects (as I personally perceive them) of coursebooks currently available in satisfying them.

In particular, I am thinking of the ambitious pupil who needs practice in the work leading to Common Entrance and Scholarship examinations to Independent Senior Schools. This book is, however, also aimed at those interested in achieving a high-level pass at GCSE, and may be used to give such pupils a comprehensive reference and set of practice exercises in Y9 and Y10. The unparalleled range of vocabulary and areas of experience now exploited by many current coursebooks will be complemented by the 'complete picture' approach I have tried to present in these pages.

Many coursebooks, though perfectly wonderful in all the right communicative ways, still give the impression of not being all that up-front about grammar. I agree wholeheartedly with the aim of getting pupils to speak before all else, but I feel that, alongside this, runs a need for clear progression through the various grammatical and structural skills that used to be evident in more traditional works. This is decidedly NOT a textbook, but I have arranged what I consider the important grammar in Part One, in a way which means that points can be checked off and briefly practised to ensure a practical level of understanding.

The book may be used in the classroom, for revision, or for private study; and I expect it to be of most value in the approach to any of the above exams. The more able pupil, looking ahead to French after GCSE, will also find it useful for revision and filling in gaps in his/her knowledge.

I have varied the 'scholarship' material as much as possible, while keeping to the disciplines most widely used at present, such as reading comprehension.

National Curriculum Areas of Experience

The areas of experience most recently proposed for Modern Foreign Languages are all addressed, to varying degrees, in this book:

A.	Everyday activities	Language of the classroom; home life and school routine; free time and leisure
B.	Personal and social life.	Self, family and friends; health and fitness; personal relationships and social activities
C.	The World around us.	Home and local region; travel and transport; life in other countries and communities
D.	The World of work.	Education and training; careers and employment
E.	The World of Communications	Newspapers and Magazines; radio and television;advertising and publicity.
F.	The international World	Tourism; customs and institutions

While some scholarship work does touch on 'business, industry , commerce and public service', these are not featured in any great depth, so they are excluded from the above list: although the topic area 'global issues and events' is also absent, certain passages in the example question papers could be said to come under that title.

(Source: "Modern Foreign Languages in the National Curriculum: Draft proposals, May 1994", School Curriculum and Assessment Authority, London. SCAA/Central Office of Information 05/94)

What this book is not

As I have pointed out, this book is not a text book, and could not really be used to replace a course book. It is not, essentially, an Oral or Listening practice book, although reference is made to these important disciplines.

Finally, it does not include a full vocabulary list - merely a collection of the more demanding words and expressions to be found within these pages.

How to use this book

Part One is a résumé of the grammar needed for Common Entrance and scholarship exams. It covers all that is needed for GCSE as well. It should be used as a reference work, to check when necessary on a particular point. If an explanation provided in Part One is not fully understood, care should be taken to make sure that the student is conversant with the terms used, and that any cross-references have been looked up.

The author has assumed throughout:
  a) that use of this book will be guided by a teacher or
       other suitably experienced person;
  b) that anyone using the book will have studied
       French for at least two years at school at least;
  c) that the book will be used as an additional extra to
       any course book.

Part Two is a carefully graded series of practice papers designed to exercise and develop the skills required for success in the above exams. The emphasis in Part Two is on encouraging the student to think about what is being tested in a particular exam question, to recognize what is required, and to proceed efficiently to a satisfactory answer. Each practice paper is shorter than most exam papers, so that the work may be used in lessons or as homework.

The practice papers include:
  a) questions and passages of text, of the types likely
       to be found in the above exams;
  b) skill-based work relevant *even if exam styles change;*
  c) a progression from pre-Common Entrance work through to
       scholarship to independent senior schools.

The work in Part Two also includes advice on technique in some of the Oral parts of these papers.

LIBRARY OF QUALITY IN EDUCATION

The basic premise of the Quality in Education series is to make available to teachers, pupils and their parents excellent resource material for the ultimate benefit of the pupils. The resource material in these books can be used to navigate the child to work from the average level to the outstanding level. The books are full of material which provide challenging exercises and enable the pupils to achieve "horizontal" proficiency in learning, ie proficiency based on the level of knowledge that a pupil is expected to have, but extending the application of the knowledge to more challenging situations.

General Editor
February 1995

ABOUT THE AUTHOR

Nigel Pearce is head of Modern Languages at Summer Fields in Oxford, and has spent practically all his working life teaching in preparatory schools. An unapologetic enthusiast for French, especially in getting children to *speak* the language, he has never exclusively adopted any one teaching 'method', preferring instead to develop a mixed style over the years.

His desire to raise the profile of French where he has taught led to the production of several French drama evenings (first developing the idea at Parkside, in Surrey, he pursued and refined it at Bramcote School, Nottinghamshire, in collaboration with St Hugh's School, Lincolnshire), in which pupils performed home-written sketches for parents, some of whom actually understood what was going on! But alongside the more active, transactional French, the need for pupils to have a clear idea of the *structure* of the language is one influence that led to the writing of this book and its eventual format.

The author lives with his wife, dog (Dudley) and cat (Aristotle), in Oxford during terms time, and in France during the holidays. His interest, apart from languages, include jazz, drawing, painting and reading.

⁓ Table des Matières ⁓

— **Deuxième Partie** —

PART ONE

GRAMMAR & STRUCTURES

1. Revision of -er Verbs

Chant-e / es / e   chant-ons / ez / ent   (i.e. basic stem + endings)

J'aime arriver dans la salle de classe le matin, où je retrouve mes copains
(I like arriving in the classroom in the morning, where I see all my friends
again).

Exercise 1 - a

Copy and complete these sentences:

1. Nous aim_____ arriver dans la salle de classe.
2. Tu arriv_____ vers quelle heure?
3. Vous retrouv_____ vos amis.
4. Tous les copains, ils chant_____ 'Alouette'.
5. Je quitt_____ l'école à cinq heures.

Exercise 1 - b

Make five sentences similar to the ones above, using the verbs given. Make
sure you take off the -er and put on the right endings.

chercher	to look for	regarder	to look at
tourner	to turn	compter	to count
écouter	to listen to		

Use a different personal pronoun in each of your sentences. Use words you
have learnt before, to do with the classroom, in your sentences

2. Ne...pas   How to say 'not' in French

Making verb expressions negative.

She swims   >   She doesn't swim.

Moi, je joue du piano, mais je ne joue pas bien.
(I play the piano, but I don't play well).

    NOTE: C'est (It is)   >   Ce n'est pas (It isn't)

When you have an apostrophe-word like *j'* or *c'* before a verb, it goes back to its full spelling before *ne,* which then becomes *n'.*

Exercise 2 - a

Make these sentences negative, by adding *'ne (verb) pas':*
1. Ma mère adore la musique.
2. Les copains de Georges dessinent leur maison.
3. Elle nage dans la mer.
4. Papa stationne la voiture du bon côté.
5. L'agent de police écoute papa.

Exercise 2 - b

Write five or more sentences of your own, taking words from the first exercises in the book if you wish: each of your sentences must be NEGATIVE. It must use 'ne (verb) pas' correctly.

Here are some more verbs to help you think up sentences:

trouver	to find	détester	to hate
durer	to last	oublier	to forget
porter	to wear		

3. Position of Adjectives.

Mostly: (Noun, then Adjective) Une *histoire* <u>incroyable</u>, un *drapeau* <u>vert</u>.

Sometimes:La <u>méchante</u> <u>petite</u> *fille* entre dans sa <u>belle</u> *maison*.   (Adjective first)

The latter are usually to do with size or character, but this is NOT a reliable rule. The following reminds us which Adjectives come BEFORE:

> Mauvais, méchant, vilain, beau
> Petit, haut, vieux, joli, gros.
> Nouveau, gentil, jeune et bon,
> Grand et meilleur, vaste et long.*

*(Watson, La Langue des Français, 1ère Partie, Harrap 1965)

Exercise 3 - a

Copy, placing the Adjective correctly:

1. J'adore marcher sur <u>l'avenue</u>   (longue)
        (l'avenue is feminine)
2. Il habite une <u>maison</u>   (blanche)
3. Elle monte sur la <u>mobylette</u> de Pierre   (neuve)
        (neuf/ neuve = new)
4. Tout le monde aime la <u>cuisine</u> de France   (délicieuse)
5. La <u>tour</u> s'appelle 'La Tour de la Lanterne'   (haute)

Exercise 3 - b

Here are some nouns. Write an appropriate Adjective to go with each one.

Example: La leçon   >   La leçon intéressante.

une voiture   un garçon   le bâtiment (building)
une émission (t.v. or radio programme) un appartement

Here are some Adjectives:

chic (smart)   ancien   rapide
ennuyeux (m) / ennuyeuse (f) (boring)   sympa (nice, kind)

There are one or two reliable rules about adjectives:

a) Adjectives of <u>colour</u> are placed after the noun.
b) Whatever their position, adjectives always agree with the noun they describe.

4. Agreement of Adjectives (basic)

Adjectives 'agree' with the nouns they describe by adding *-s* in the plural and
-e in the feminine. In the feminine plural *-es* is added:

Une excellente journé<u>e</u>   Des films comique<u>s</u>

Exercise 4 - a

Copy these Adjectives, writing alongside them their other three forms: Masculine plural; Feminine singular and Feminine plural.

Example: excellent   excellents   excellente   excellentes

1. amusant   2. bruyant   3. grand   4. plein
5. petit   6. court (short) 7. étroit (narrow)
8. rond   9. chaud   10. froid

Learn the ones whose meanings you didn't know.

Exercise 4 - b

Now write a few phrases, each of which contains an Adjective, in the correct position and with the correct ending.

5. le, la, les used as Direct Object Pronouns.

Tu vois le cinéma? > Tu le vois?

le = him/it   la = her/it   les = them

NOTE the position of 'le' in the above sentence. Direct Object Pronouns usually go before the 'working' verb (the one that goes with the person).
When there is an infinitive (and common sense tells you that the pronoun makes sense next to it) it goes before the Infinitive:

Elle veut voir (wants to see) le film. > Elle veut **le** voir.

In this example, 'it' OBVIOUSLY goes with 'to see' rather than '<u>wants</u>'.
le and *la* change to *l'* [as normal] before a vowel: Je *l'*aime.

Exercise 5 - a

Rewrite these sentences, replacing the object words with pronouns:
1.   Marguerite cherche le foulard.
2.   Tu retrouves les amis.
3.   Marc et Jeanne oublient le magazine.
4.   Philippe veut regarder le tableau.
5.   Nous allons rendre les cahiers au professeur.

6. Aller   to go   to be going

From now on, it will be assumed that you know the order in which verbs are set out (je, tu, il/elle/on, nous, vous, ils/elles), and that the THIRD PERSON singular of all verbs is the same for <u>elle</u> and <u>on</u> as it is for <u>il</u>. The same is true about <u>elles</u> and <u>ils</u>.

Verbs will therefore be set out as follows:

vais	allons
vas	allez
va	vont

Exercise 6 - a

Make sentences out of the following phrases, by adding part of Aller. Your sentences will express where someone is going.

1. à la cantine
2. au dortoire
3. chez le directeur
4. au gymnase
5. aux vestiaires

Give the English for these completed sentences.

Aller is also used with Infinitives to express the Future: to be going to...

Exercise 6 - b

Give the French for:
1. We're going to eat.
2. She's going to arrive.
3. You're going to forget.
4. Then make up two examples of your own and give the English for them.

7. Vouloir   to want   Pouvoir   to be able

These verbs are very similar in some ways:

veux	voulons	peux	pouvons
veux	voulez	peux	pouvez
veut	veulent	peut	peuvent

They are very often followed by Infinitives:

Je veux trouver ma calculatrice (I want <u>to find</u> my calculator).

Exercise 7 - a

Write five sentences using *vouloir* and five using *pouvoir*, with the following Infinitive phrases after them:
1. arriver à temps (to arrive on time)
2. vérifier mon emploi du temps (to check my timetable)
3. rentrer en classe (to go back into lessons) *
4. être reçu à l'examen (to pass the exam)
5. assister au concert (to be present at the concert)
6. jouer de la flûte (play the flute)
7. compter en français
8. sauter plus loin que toi (jump further than you!)
9. taper au clavier (type on the keyboard)
10. parler italien (speak Italian).

* You could use this one in the negative! (Make vouloir negative before adding the Infinitive).

8. En   used to mean « of it » or « of them ».

Il y a combien d'ordinateurs à ton école? > Il y en a trente.

'En' is in that position because 'a' is the verb.
You cannot leave 'en' out in French.

Exercise 8 - a

Rewrite these sentences, using 'en' instead of the underlined parts:
1. Georges a cinq feutres (felt-tip pens).
2. Philippe achète un kilo de beurre .
3. Je lis (read) deux des livres.
4. Nous rencontrons (meet) une vingtaine (about 20) d'étudiants.
5. Vous vendez (sell) des timbres?

NOTE: 'DE' can also mean 'From', so 'En can mean 'from it' / 'from them'.

9. Me, te, nous, vous as Direct Object Pronouns.

Tu m'écoutes.   Il te regarde.   Vous nous enseignez.
(You listen to me. He's watching you. You teach us.)

Exercise 9 - a

Look at Grammar Points 5, 6, 7, 8 and 9 again, then express in French:
1. She looks at us.
2. We teach you (s).
3. They meet us.
4. I'm watching you (pl).
5. He sells them. (sells = vend)

Exercise 9 - b

Try these, which have Infinitives:
1. They want to meet you (s).   (to meet = rencontrer)
2. She can't forget them.
3. I don't want to wear it (f).
4. Jeanne wants to draw her.   (to draw = dessiner)
5. Michel and Sylvain can count them.

10. Falloir Only used with 'il': Il faut (It is necessary).

NOTE: its uses compared with English:

Il faut partir. It is necessary to go (We'd better go, etc.)
Il ne faut pas se disputer. One shouldn't argue.

This expression is used to show that someone needs something:

Il nous faut une règle. (We need a ruler).

The 'nous' here means 'to us': It is necessary 'to us'.

NOTE: To say 'It is necessary TO HIM/TO HER', use: lui:
To say 'It is necessary TO THEM, use: leur:

21

Il lui faut des crayons: He/She needs pencils.
Il leur faut sortir: They need to go out

Exercise 10 - a

Express in English:
1. Il nous faut de nouveaux cahiers, Monsieur.
2. Il me faut arriver avant (before) six heures.
3. Il ne faut pas écrire dans les livres.
4. Il faut écouter.
5. Il leur faut faire attention! (What do you think 'faire attention' means?)

Exercise 10 - b

Write these expressions in French:
1. She ought to pay attention.
2. We need some exercise books.
3. They need rulers.
4. One shouldn't play in the classroom.
5. You need some pens.

11. Pronouns - Reprise

I	me	to me	myself	me (strong)
etc	*etc*	*etc*	*etc*	*etc*
je	me	me	me	moi
tu	te	te	te	toi
il	le	lui	se	lui
elle	la	lui	se	elle
on		se		soi
nous	nous	nous	nous	nous
vous	vous	vous	vous	vous
ils	les	leur	se	eux
elles	les	leur	se	elles

Exercise 11 - a

Start thinking in a different way: there may seem to be many pronouns, but in fact only a few are *different* words. The total of *different* pronouns is 10, or 16 if you include 'y' (there/ to it/ in that place) and 'en' (see 8) and *moi, toi, soi, eux*. All the rest are repeated.

Pronouns going BEFORE the verb:

me	te	se	nous	vous
	le	la	les	
	lui	leur		
	y	en		

Your task is to learn these IN THIS ORDER, BY HEART.

Exercise 11 - b

Pronouns coming AFTER the verb. This only happens in Commands:

Ecoutez-moi. Donnez-le-moi. Allez-y!

The ORDER to learn BY HEART is:

moi		
le	toi	
la	lui	y
les	leur	en
nous		
vous		

Exercise 11 - c

Rewrite these sentences, correctly placing the right French pronouns.
Where there are more than one, the order you have just learnt is the order they go in.
1. Tu envoies (=send) [it(f) to him].
2. Elle aime [them].

    3. Nous essayons téléphoner [you pl]. (Spotted the Infinitive?!)
    4. Il donne [them to us].
    5. Rendez [it(m) to me!].

When the Command is Negative, (DON'T do something) the order is the same as in the first triangle, Exercise 11 - a.

Exercise 11 - d

Rewrite these negative commands with the right pronouns in the right places.
1. Ne cherche pas la balle.
2. N'allons pas à la pâtisserie.
3. Ne cachez pas les papiers.

Exercise 11 - e

Make up 2 more negative commands of your own with pronouns.

12. Plurals: Nouns and Adjectives whose singulars end in s, x or z.

Most Nouns and Adjectives end in -s in the Plural. Those nouns which end in -s, -x, or -z in the Singular DO NOT CHANGE in the Plural:

les nez rouges des clowns: the clowns' red noses.

Exercise 12

Rewrite these phrases in the plural:
1. Le choix (choice) difficile.
2. Le grand Anglais (the tall Englishman).
3. Le dos courbé (the bent back).
4. Le cours de maths.
5. Le petit roux (the little red-haired boy).

13. Faire meaning: to do   or: to make.

fais   faisons
fais   FAITES   Notice the unusual Vous - form.
fait   font

Faire is very common in French. It is used with many weather expressions and, in phrases, to express certain activities (e.g. *faire* la vaisselle, to do the washing-up).

14. Dire and Lire. Two rather similar but different Irregular Verbs.

Dire, to say   Lire, to read

dis   disons   lis   lisons
dis   DITES   lis   lisez
dit   disent   lit   lisent

If you want to say 'TELL' (rather than SAY), you have to 'Say TO people'.

Exercise 14 - a

Express in French:
1. She says.
2. We say to Jean.
3. Paul says.
4. I'm reading.
5. They're telling them.
6. They tell her.
7. She tells me.
8. Tell me!
9. You don't read (s).
10. Are you (pl) reading?

14 / bis: Telling people to do things:

We use the verb « Dire », as explained above, for telling as well as saying. This includes telling people to do things. But in French we have to 'Say TO someone to do something':

Je dis à Paul DE téléphoner ce soir (I tell Paul to phone tonight).

The construction is: Dire à (someone) DE +Infinitive (Don't forget DE!)

...which means that, when we use Pronouns instead of Nouns or names, we have to use the ones meaning to him; to you, etc. (see 11 above to check):

Je leur dis de vérifier le prix (I tell them to check the price).

Finally, what is true for « Dire » in this respect, is also true for:

Demander (to ask); Proposer (to suggest); Persuader; Inviter;
Défendre (to forbid); Promettre [like Mettre] (to promise)
...and some others you will come across.

15. Transport Methods: When to use à and en.

Elle arrive *en* voiture, mais elle repart (sets off again) *à* vélo.

EN: When you are IN an enclosed conveyance (e.g. car; aeroplane)
A : When you are ON / OUTSIDE an open form of transport (e.g. bicycle).

Exercise 15 - a

Complete with the correct preposition à or en:
1. On va à Boulogne (...) car-ferry.
2. Thierry va aller à l'hôpital (...) bicyclette.
3. Nous revenons (...) autobus.
4. Je vais au bureau (...) métro.
5. Ma tante arrive ce matin (...) car.

16. Future Simple Tense (le Futur Simple)

Quand j'aurai treize ans, je changerai d'école.

The tense that means 'will' or 'shall'. Most verbs have regular Future formation:
Infinitive up to the last 'r' (Vendr-; tomber-) and add:

$$ai, \quad as, \quad a, \quad ons, \quad ez, \quad ont.$$

(Like avoir in the Present Tense but without av-)

There are quite a lot of irregular stems (but all ENDINGS are regular).

		Future
acheter	>	achèter- (buy)
envoyer	>	enverr- (send)
essuyer	>	essuier- (wipe)*

* and all verbs in -uyer and -oyer except envoyer and renvoyer (to send back)

appeler	>	appeller-(call) and rappeler
jeter	>	jetter-(throw)
mener	>	mèner-(lead) and its derivatives
avoir	>	aur-(have)
être	>	ser-(be)
faire	>	fer-(do, make)
aller	>	ir-(go)
pouvoir	>	pourr- (be able)
vouloir	>	voudr-(want)
falloir	>	faudr-(be necessary)
valoir	>	vaudr- (be worth)
venir, tenir	>	viendr-, tiendr- (come, hold)
recevoir, devoir	>	recevr-, devr-(receive, have to)
savoir	>	saur-(know [a fact])
courir	>	courr-(run)
mourir	>	mourr-(die)

16. Future Tense continued.

NOTE that falloir and valoir are only use with 'il'.
This is also true of: pleuvoir (to rain) > pleuvr-
LEARN the above irregular futures. As you come to new verbs, learn whether they have irregular futures or not, and, if so, commit them to MEMORY.

Exercise 16 - a

Copy and complete, writing the verbs in brackets in the Futur Simple tense:
1. On (arriver) avant midi.
2. Ils (jouer) au tennis cet après-midi.

   3. Nous (avoir) froid ici.
   4. J'espère qu'il (faire) beau demain.
   5. Est-ce que tu (aller) en Italie l'année prochaine?

Exercise 16 - b

Write down the verb which each of these Future expressions comes from:

1.	Elle viendra.	4.	Tu iras.
2.	Nous deviendrons.	5.	Vous aurez.
3.	Je serai.		

Exercise 16 - c

Give the English for Exercise 16 - b Nos. 1 to 5.

17. Comparing the Futur Simple with Aller plus Infinitive.

Elle va me demander quel temps il fera demain.
(She's going to ask me what the weather will be like tomorrow.)

Aller : vais allons
         vas   allez
         va   vont

is the same as the English 'to be going to...'whereas the Futur is nearer to 'will'.

Exercise 17 - a

Write (1) four phrases using the Futur, giving the weather forecast.
Verbs you need: faire; neiger; pleuvoir (Fut. Stem: pleuvr-); être.

Write (2) four phrases using Aller + Infinitive, saying what you are going to do tomorrow.

18. Using « à » and « de ».

A huit heures / à Paris	//	De soie / de Lyon
At 8 o'clock / in Paris	//	Of silk / from Lyon

(à Paris can also mean 'to Paris'). Study these other examples:

(a) Using « de »:

OF: .   une tranche de jambon, cinq kilos de sucre.
'S: la voiture de mon cousin, la copine de Pierre-Yves.
FROM: Il vient de Paris. C'est une lettre de Marc.

Lastly, to use one NOUN to describe another:

une rue de village, mes affaires (stuff, things) de classe.

(b) Using « *à* »:

TO   Ce soir on va aller à Joinville en voiture.
AT   Elle restera à la maison, comme d'habitude (as usual).
IN   Nous dînerons à Paris.

Lastly, « à » is used sometimes to denote attributes or possession:

C'est à qui? (Whose is it?) – C'est à moi!.
Je vais acheter une voiture à trois roues (wheels).

NOTE: Whether you use *à* or *de* can make the difference between a QUANTITY of something, or the PURPOSE of the item:

un verre A vin (a wine glass); un verre DE vin (a glass of wine).

Exercise 18 - a

Choose between *à* and *de* and copy, inserting the correct one:
1.   Les véhicules (...) quatre roues sont interdits.
2.   La chaîne (hi-fi) (...) ma soeur est en panne.
3.   Il faudra trois paquets (...) biscuits.
4.   La trousse bleue? Elle est (...) Jean-Paul.
5.   Je prend un bol (...) café tous les matins.

Exercise 18 - b

Write 5 sentences or phrases of your own, in which *à* and *de* are used differently each time.

19. A and DE used with le, la, l', les:

Au village, prenez la direction du Camping des Anges.
(At the village, take the turning to the Camping des Anges).

Masculine Singular	:	à + le = au	de + le = du
Feminine Singular	:	à + la = à la	de + la = de la
Sing. before a vowel	:	à + l' = à l'	de + l' = de l'
Plural (m/f)	:	à + les = aux	de + les = des

Exercise 19 - a

Copy, replacing English with the correct French:
1. (to the) parents (of) Paul.
2. (of the) maire (m) de notre village.
3. (to) Le Havre [watch out!].
4. (at) Le Mans.
5. (to the) amis (of the) docteur.

Exercise 19 - b

Write one of the above (au, du etc.) with each of these, then give the English for your phrase: check whether they are *m.* or *f.*

père, médecin, cuisines, lapin, jambes, frères, soeur, cassette, pain, jupe hôtel, arbres, cour, église, planche à roulettes.

20. Verbs requiring *à* or *de.*

There are several common verb expressions which are followed by *à* and *de*:

Il essaie DE me tromper: He tries to trick me.
On commence A s'inquiéter: We're starting to get worried.

NOTE that in each case the second verb is an INFINITIVE.

apprendre à	(to learn to)
commencer à	(to begin to)
continuer à	(to continue, to carry on ...ing)
se mettre à	(to begin to)
s'occuper à	(to be busy ...ing)
servir à	(to be used for)
s'intéresser à	(to be interested in ...ing)
s'arrêter de	(to stop)
cesser de	(to stop)
décider de	(to decide to)
demander de	(to ask someone to)
essayer de	(to try to)
faire semblant de	(to pretend to)
oublier de	(to forget to)
permettre de	(to allow to)
promettre de	(to promise to)
refuser de	(to refuse to)
remercier de	(to thank for)

Exercise 20 - a

Copiez et complétez en français:
1. Il essaie (..) finir à temps.
2. Quand est-ce que tu vas commencer (..) écrire cette lettre?
3. Je promets (..) te téléphoner demain.
4. Sophie s'intéresse (..) faire de la musique.
5. Il est temps que l'on se met (..) répéter.

Exercise 20 - b

Traduisez les phrases ci-dessus [above] en anglais.

21. Irregular (Masculines and) Feminines of Adjectives.

La vieille souris blanche est mignonne, n'est-ce pas?

Adjective	Meaning	Before Vowel (m)	Feminine
beau	nice to look at, fine etc.	bel	belle
vieux	old (not young)	vieil	vieille
nouveau	new	nouvel	nouvelle
gros	big		grosse
gras	fat/ greasy		grasse
gentil	kind, nice		gentille
actif	active		active
vif	lively, sharp		vive
neuf	(brand) new		neuve
mignon	cute, sweet		mignonne
blanc	white		blanche
doux	quiet, gentle, sweet-tasting		douce
bas	low		basse

Other irregular adjectives will appear during the book: learn them as they come up.

Exercise 21 - a

Copiez et complétez, en vous servant de la forme correcte de l'adjectif:
1. Le (handsome) homme monte dans son (new) avion.
2. Madame Delacroix devient (fat).
3. La (old) dame est très (kind) avec moi.

Exercise 21 - b

Inventez et écrivez 5 exemples avec 5 adjectifs irréguliers différents.

22. Another Pronoun note.

So far, you have looked at:

Direct Object (me); Indirect Object (to me); Reflexive (myself) and the so-called 'strong' pronouns have been mentioned. A word or two about them:

They are called 'strong' because they stand alone and do not need the 'support' of a verb.

They are the ones you find after PREPOSITIONS and on their own.

Elle va partir avec lui?   Non, elle va partir avec <u>moi</u>!
(Is she going to leave with him?   No, she's going to leave with me!)

In each of these, the Preposition is AVEC (with). Here are some more examples:

sans elle	without her	avant nous	before us
derrière eux	behind them (m)	après vous	after you
malgré moi	despite me	auprès de toi	near you
chez lui	at his house ('at-the-house-of him')	selon elles	according to them

Qui a fait ce dessin?   Moi, monsieur!
Who did this drawing?   Me, sir!

Exercise 22 - a

Essayez de penser à 5 exemples où des Prépositions sont suivis de ces pronoms. (Try to think of 5 examples where Prepositions are followed by these pronouns).

23. Etre   to be

Je suis français, mais elles sont américaines; et toi, tu es anglais?

suis	sommes
es	êtes
est	sont

One of the most important Verbs in the language, ETRE must be learnt by heart immediately if you haven't done it already. Its English is pretty irregular too:

am	are
are	are
is	are

...so don't think French is alone in having irregular verbs!

Exercice 23 - a

Copiez et complétez:
Je (....) Philippe. Sophie (...) ma soeur, et Paul et Marie-Claire
(...) mes parents. Nous (...) français. Et vous, vous (...) d'ici?
Mon copain Asim n'(...) pas d'ici: lui et son frère Asif (...) Omanais.

Exercice 23 - b

Inventez un petit paragraphe comme celui de l'Exercice 23 - a.

24. *Ce (Cet) Cette* [this / that]; *Ces* [these / those]

Ce bâtiment est encore plus beau que cette maison neuve.
That building is even nicer than that new house.

Singular Masculine :	Ce. Masculine before a vowel: Cet (e.g. Cet avion).
Singular Feminine :	Cette.
Plural (m/f) :	Ces

Exercice 24

Mettez la forme correcte de ce / cet / cette / ces devant ces mots:

1. animal
2. voitures
3. hommes
4. magnétoscope (m)
5. jupe
6. sortie
7. cafetière (f).

25. Avoir   to have

At least as important as Etre, AVOIR must be known by heart as well:

ai	avons
as	avez
a	ont

It features in many expressions where English does NOT say 'have', so it is not all that straight forward:

J'ai peur   -   I'm afraid. (I HAVE fear)

There are many more of these in Note 59.

Exercice 25 - a

Copiez et complétez:
Moi, j'(...) un cousin qui (...) trois frères. Moi, j'(...) un frère, donc, ensemble, ça fait que nous en (...) quatre. Et toi, tu (...) des frères? Les frères de mon cousin (...) des vélos tout-terrain.

Exercice 25 - b

Ecrivez un paragraphe comme celui de l'Exercice 24 - a

26. Prendre to take (also: to 'have' = to eat/drink)

prends	prenons
prends	prenez
prend	prennent

Mettre to put (also: to put ON - clothing, etc.)

mets	mettons
mets	mettez
met	mettent

Exercice 26 - a

Copiez et complétez, en vous servant de la forme correcte du verbe:
1. En rentrant à la maison, je (take) une douche.
2. Marc (puts) une cassette et on l'écoute.
3. On (has) le déjeuner vers une heure et demie.
4. Maman et tante Elizabeth (put on) leur gros manteau.
5. Vous (are taking) quel avion, monsieur?

Exercice 26 - b

Traduisez toutes les phrases de l'Exercice 26 - a en anglais.

27. Negative : *Ne ... rien*

Tu ne manges rien; tu ne dis rien; voilà tout ce que tu fais: rien!
(You don't eat anything; you don't say anything; that's all you do: nothing!)

'*Ne...rien*' is used like: 'Ne...pas', with *NE* before the verb and *Rien* after it:

Tu ne manges PAS	:	You don't eat.
Tu ne manges RIEN	:	You eat NOTHING
		(or You don't eat anything).

Exercice 27 - a

Ecrivez 5 phrases, en vous servant de « ..(verbe)..rien » et des   indications (clues) ci-dessous (below):

Exemple: Vous - faites   >   Vous ne faites rien.

1. Tu - lis.
2. On - apprend.
3. Nous - avons.
4. Il - écrit.
5. Philippe et Simon - comprennent.

Exercice 27 - b

Traduisez vos phrases en anglais.

28. Irregular *-ER* Verbs: Acheter; Jeter; Appeler

These are widely-used examples of -ER Verbs whose endings are normal, but whose STEMS change their spelling when the ENDING is UNPRONOUNCED*:

Acheter   to buy

achète   achetons (pronounced)
achètes   achetez (pronounced)
achète   achètent

Some verbs make a change, not by adding an accent grave , but by doubling the letter before the endings:

Jeter   to throw   Appeler   to call

jette   jetons   appelle   appelons
jettes   jetez   appelles   appelez
jette   jettent   appelle   appellent

Have you noticed what these verbs have in common? It is that the last few letters of their infinitives are: E + CONSONANT + ER (-eler, -eter, etc.).

All derivatives of LEVER and MENER do the same as Acheter.

LEARN these (and when they change *) so you can apply the rule to similar verbs.

Exercice 28

Donnez la forme correcte de:

1. Tu te (lever).
2. On se (promener).
3. Je (appeler).
4. Elles (soulever).
5. Ils (rappeler).
6. Nous (ammener).
7. Vous (ramener).
8. Tu te (rappeler).

29. Revision of My, His/Her/One's, Your.

Masculine Singular:	Mon*	Son*	Ton*
Feminine Singular:	Ma	Sa	Ta
Plural (m/f):	Mes	Ses	Tes

Reminder No.1*: Before FEM/SINGULAR nouns beginning with VOWEL, use MON, TON, SON (instead of MA etc.):

A school   Une école.   MY school MON école.

Reminder No. 2: The words for HIS/HER/ONE'S do not work the same way as in English.

John looks after (<)HIS guitar. (HIS because JOHN is Masc.)
John soigne SA (>) guitare. (SA because GUITARE is Fem.)

Reminder No. 3: You can only use TON etc. for YOUR if you are using TU for YOU.

Vous adorez TON chat   .. is wrong.
Tu adores TON chat   .. is right.
(For vous, use VOTRE and the plural VOS for YOUR: Vous adorez VOTRE chat .. is now right!)

Exercice 29 - a

Traduisez en français:
1. her father.
2. one's pen.
3. your aunt.
4. his mum.
5. her cars.
6. your uncle.

Exercice 29 - b

Ecrivez six phrases avec des adjectifs de possession (mon, ton etc.), et donnez-en l'anglais. (...and give the English for them).

30. Revision of Our and Your (when using Vous).

Have you noticed that Nous begins with N, and so do Notre and Nos?
Have you noticed that Vous begins with V, and so do Votre and Vos?
That should remind you that they go together:

We /Our : Nous	>	NOTRE (singular) ;	NOS (Plural).
You /Your : Vous	>	VOTRE (S.) ;	VOS (Pl.)

Exercice 30

Traduisez en français:
1. Our Father
2. Your sisters.
3. Our swimming-pool
4. Your house.
5. Our trees.
6. Your friends.

31. Venir to come

This Irregular Verb forms the pattern for many others, which copy it in very nearly all its tenses. The most important are:

Tenir - to hold;   Revenir - to come back;
Devenir - to become   Venir: to come

viens	venons
viens	venez
vient	viennent

Exercice 31 - a

Exprimez (express) en français:
1. They come back.   4. She's holding.
2. You (pl) are coming.   5. I become.
3. They (f) hold.

Exercice 31 - b

See if you can write out all the parts of *devenir* from memory. If you can't, you need to LEARN these verbs again until you can.

32. Dormir   to sleep

Just like the one above, *dormir* is an important pattern-verb for a handful of other, very widely-used Verbs.These are:

Partir	to leave / depart / go away
Sortir	to go out / get (something) out (from somewhere)
Sentir	to sense / feel
Servir	to serve
Mentir	to lie / tell a lie / be lying.

Dormir: Try to notice its pattern. It uses its first 3 letters in the
Singular parts; and its first 4 in the Plural parts.

dors	dormons	(DOR s ; DORM ons)
dors	dormez	
dort	dorment.	

Sortir (for example) doesn't have an 'M' as its 4th letter, but a 'T', so its Nous - part will *not* be Nous SORMons but Nous *SORTons*.

Exercice 32 - a

Essayez de découvrir toutes les formes correctes de:
1. Partir   (Je pars, tu pars, etc.)
2. Servir
3. Sentir
4. Mentir.
5. Sortir.

Exercice 32 - b

Choisissez cinq exemples de ce que vous venez d'écrire et traduisez-les en anglais. (Choose five examples from what you have just written ...)

33. Voir   to see

vois	voyons
vois	voyez
voit	voient

34. Irregular -*ER* Verbs: Nettoyer, to clean; Essayer, to try; Envoyer, to send.
(See Note 28 to refresh your memory about 'Irregular' -ER Verbs).

Essayer:

essaie	essayons
essaies	essayez
essaie	essaient

Exercices 33 et 34

Copiez et complétez:
1. On y va en taxi - c'est maman qui (payer)!
2. Louis (essuyer) le tableau pour le professeur.
3. Si tu ne (voir) pas Éric, c'est qu'il (nettoyer) sa chambre.
4. Nous (essayer) de finir ces notes avant minuit.
5. Elle m'(envoyer) une carte tous les ans pour ma fête.

35. Countries: Masculine and Feminine; Whether to use 'à' or 'en'.

The names in French of most countries are FEMININE:

L'Angleterre	La France	La Belgique
L'Italie	La Suède	La Suisse
L'Allemagne	La Bosnie	La Serbie
La Russie	La Pologne	La Tchétchénie
L'Espagne	L'Autriche	La Croatie

With these, to say IN or TO the country, use « EN »:

En Angleterre, en Bosnie, en Croatie, etc.

The names of many important nations are, however, masculine.
Some Masculine names of Countries:

Le Japon   Le Canada   Le Portugal   Le Maroc

Some are Plural: Les Etats Unis (U.S.A)

For the Masculines, to say IN or TO the country, use « AU »:

Au Maroc,   au Canada,   au Portugal

For the Plurals, use « AUX »:Aux Etats Unis, aux Antilles (in / to the WestIndies).

Exercice 35

Exprimez en français:
1. In China   (China = La Chine)
2. In Spain
3. To Japan
4. To Serbia
5. In Germany

36.   Chez + People's names and 'strong' Pronouns.

Cet après-midi, si on passait chez Jean-Michel?
(This afternoon, why don't we go to Jean-Michel's?)

Chez is used to mean 'to the house of' or 'at the house of'.

It is most important to think of it in this way, since many mistakes are made when it is used the wrong way:

To Michel's house (= TO-THE-HOUSE-OF Michel) = CHEZ Michel.

So there's no need for the word 'maison', of course. This also means that, when using expressions like 'to MY house', in French we use CHEZ with a Strong Pronoun:

At MY house (= AT-THE-HOUSE-OF me) = CHEZ moi.

The word CHEZ also means: At/To-the-place-of-work-of and is found in such expressions as:

Je dois aller chez le dentiste;
Ma mère travaille chez John Lewis, etc.

It can denote sections of the community, or peoples:

On trouve ces croyances (beliefs) chez les Incas.

Exercice 36 - a

Exprimez en français:
1. At her house. (See note 11 above, for Strong Pronouns).
2. To his house.
3. At the chemist's
4. Among women. (Say: the women)
5. At Sainsbury's.

Exercice 36 - b

Inventez cinq expressions, en vous servant de « Chez ».

37. De (du, etc.) + Names: Expressing 'apostrophe - s'

Lui? C'est le frère d'un copain du professeur de géographie de Jules.
(Him? He's Jules's geography teacher's friend's brother.)

The above examples show how DE is used to perform the same function as 's does in English. The words 'DU' and 'DES' are therefore used for the same purpose.

Jules's brother   :   Le frère DE Jules
The teacher's friend: Le copain DU professeur.

In the first example, the word used is DE (of); in the second, it is DU (of the: See note 19).

Exercice 37 - a

Exprimez en français:
1. John's mountain bike.
2. Charlotte's CD player. (le lecteur de disques-compacts).
3. The dentist's surgery. (le cabinet).
4. Philippe's sister's perfume.

Exercice 37 - b

Trouvez cinq exemples de « de » pour exprimer l' « 's » anglais.

38. Savoir   To Know

(A fact; that something is true, etc. It does not mean to know a person or place. That it Connaître, in note 72 below).

sais	savons
sais	savez
sait	savent

39. Devoir   To Have to ('must'); to Owe

A wide-ranging verb with many uses, not always the same as in English.

dois	devons
dois	devez
doit	doivent

Il doit être huit heures.	-	It must be 8 o'clock.
Je dois partir.	-	I have to go.
Tu me dois cinq francs.	-	You owe me 5F.

Exercice 39 - a

Traduisez en français:
1. She owes them (to them!) some money.
2. We must clean our bedrooms.
3. They have to arrive before nine.
4. You (pl) don't have to know.
5. He must come with me.

Exercice 39 - b

Ecrivez cinq phrases pour pratiquer l'usage du verbe *devoir*.

40. The Imperative (L'Impératif) and Irregular Imperatives.

Venez voir notre spectacle, dînez et dansez après!
(Come and see our show, and have dinner and dance afterwards!)

(a) To make an Imperative (a command or instruction), simply use the 'you' forms of the verbs you need without 'you':

Tu viens   >   Viens! (You come > Come!)
Vous dansez   >   Dansez!

Only one problem: On any -er verb, you remove the 's' from the 'tu' ending:

Tu mélanges   >   Mélange! (Mélanger = to mix)

(b) To say 'Let's ... ' you use one further Imperative, using the 'nous' form of the verb in question:

Nous partons   >   Partons! (Let's go!)

There are only a few irregular Imperatives in French:

Savoir: Sache,   Sachons,   Sachez
Etre: Sois,   Soyons,   Soyez
Avoir: Aie,   Ayons,   Ayez

Exercice 40 - a

Dites à quelqu'un (tell someone) en français de faire ces choses:
1. (Tu) Go to the station.
2. (Vous) Wait outside (devant) the cinema.
3. Let's watch the other film.
4. (Tu) Take my car.
5.. (Tu) Put on these shoes.

Exercice 40 - b

Inventez cinq Impératifs en français et traduisez-les en anglais.

(c) Imperatives with Pronouns, and Negative Imperatives.

These are covered in Note 11, from the point of view of Pronouns.
Note the structure and order of the examples:

1. Donne-les-lui.   (Give them to him/her).
2. Ne téléphone pas ce soir.   (Don't ring tonight).
3. Ne t'en fais pas. (An expression meaning: Don't worry about it).

41. Devrait ('should') and other Devoir difficulties.

Elle devrait être là avant une heure. (She should be there by one o'clock).
Note this part of Devoir, compared with what we would say in English:

Tu devrais savoir.   You should know
                        You ought to know.

It is a tense called the conditional of Devoir. The conditional usually means
'would', so this expression could mean 'you would have to know' as well.

devrais	devrions
devrais	devriez
devrait	devraient

There will be more on the other forms of Devoir, and their meanings, later.
Devoir is followed by verbs in the Infinitive.

Exercice 41 - a

Donnez le français pour:
1. She should arrive at the restaurant at eight.
2. We (use 'on') should cross the road here.
3. They ought to answer (say 'answer to') your letter.
4. Marc shouldn't use (utiliser) that bike.
5. Shouldn't you go home now?

Exercice 41 - b

Utilisez le conditionnel de Devoir pour composer quelques phrases et traduisez-les en anglais.

42. Leur   as an Adjective, meaning: Their

You have seen « leur » as a pronoun, meaning: 'to them'.
It also means 'their' and, as an Adjective in this case, has to agree with the Noun it describes.

Note: It does not change for the Feminine, but it DOES for the Plural.

Ils donnent à manger (they give food) à LEUR chien.
Natalie et sa soeur mettent LEURS chaussures blanches.

Exercice 42

Ecrivez cinq exemples de noms (nouns) précédés de (preceded by) « leur » et cinq autres exemples où les noms sont précédés de « leurs ».

43. On

On arrive vers une heure, on se lave les mains, et on mange tout de suite.
(You arrive at 1 o'clock, you wash your hands, then you eat straight away).

On is used much more often in French than 'one', its nearest equivalent in English. The French prefer it, quite often, to « nous », and in English we tend to use several different words to express it:

On sort à huit heures.	We're going out at 8.
On dit que c'est difficile.	They say it's difficult.
On me dit que la route est bloquée.	I'm told that the road's blocked.
On fait deux ans d'études supérieures.	You do 2 years' advanced study.

Exercice 43 - a

Traduisez en anglais:
1. On prend le petit déjeuner à sept heures et demie.
2. Qu'est-ce qu'on va faire?
3. On y arrivera demain soir.
4. Quand on lit les journaux, on y trouve toujours de mauvaises nouvelles.
   (y = there).

Exercice 43 - b

Composez cinq phrases en français, où le mot « on » est employé différemment dans chaque phrase.

44. Tout: Its spellings and meanings.

Tout can be an adjective or a noun. Depending on its use, it can mean:

all   every   everything   whole   very

Quand on est tout petit   (very young)
Tout le jardin est beau   (The whole garden)
Toutes les fleurs te sourient   (every flower)
Tout paraît nouveau   (Everything)

It's also used in some very common everyday expressions:

Tout le monde   Everyone / Everybody
Tout de suite   Immediately
Tout à l'heure   Just now / In a little while

Masculine Singular: Tout M. Plural: TOUS (Note this spelling)
Feminine Singular: Toute F. Plural: Toutes

Exercice 44 - a

Traduisez en français:
1. All the boys.
2. Every skateboard (A skateboard = une planche à roulettes).
3. The whole class.
4. A very young child.
5. Everything seems old (seems = paraît).

Exercice 44 - b

Ecrivez cinq exemples de « tout » en français, puis traduisez vos exemples en anglais.

45. Le Passé Composé (1)   (The Perfect Tense using Avoir)

J'ai trouvé le mot que tu as laissé. (I found the note that you left).

Note that, for the ONE expression in French, THREE are possible in English:

* J'ai trouvé   I have found, I found (and, sometimes, I did find)

In French, 'Je trouvé' is not correct without part of Avoir: J'ai trouvé.

*The first is the same formula in English as in French:

Person	+	have	+	past participle
J'		ai		trouvé
I		have		found

The DIFFICULTY is in remembering to put part of Avoir, to express the past, however it is said in English:

I watched t.v.

Should it be: Je regardé la télé. or   J'ai regardé la télé. ?
If you don't know, read note 45 again.

Le Passé Composé des Verbes Réguliers en « -ER »:

Avoir: (ai   avons
       as   avez *plus* participe passé (e.g. manger > mang**é**)
       a   ont)

Exercice 45 - a

Ecrivez des phrases au Passé Composé, utilisant les pronoms et des verbes suivants:
(Exemple: Nous (manger) > Nous avons mangé).
1. Tu (donner) mon journal à Sylvie.
2. On (casser) une fenêtre, mademoiselle.
3. Ils (chercher) leur cahier de géographie.
4. La cousine de Claude (parler) à ses parents au téléphone.
5. Vous (raccrocher). [Raccrocher = to put the phone down].

Exercice 45 - b

Traduisez ces phrases en anglais.

46. Boire   to drink

bois	buvons
bois	buvez
boit	boivent

Past Participle:	bu.	
Passé Composé:	j'ai bu	nous avons bu
	tu as bu	vous avez bu
	il a bu	ils ont bu

47. Expressing 'How Often' things happen.

Je prends un casse-croûte tous les matins à onze heures.
(I have a snack every morning at eleven).

Tous les / Toutes les (m / f) = Every

Question: Tu écris à tes parents tous les combien? (= how often?)
Réponse :   Normalement, toutes les semaines.

tous les mardi
toutes les deux heures
tous les jours à partir de 17 h*
tous les jours sauf jours fériés et le dimanche*
une fois tous les trois jours (once every 3 days)
une fois par semaine (once a week)
(Une fois = once. What is 'twice'?)

*Expressions of frequency are often used on notices.

Exercice 47 - a

Traduisez en français:
1. Every evening.
2. Every afternoon.
3. How often do you go to the cinema?
4. I don't know... twice a month, perhaps.
5. Every morning from 8 o'clock.

Exercice 47 - b

Composez en français cinq autres exemples, puis traduisez-les en anglais.

48. Revision: Regular -ir Verbs in the Present Tense

remplis	remplissons
remplis	remplissez
remplit	remplissent(Remember!Don't pronounce the-nt !)

Here are some *-ir* Verbs you may remember, and some you may not have met yet:

grandir	to get taller
grossir	to get big / fat
élargir	to widen
blanchir	to whiten (la blanchisserie - the laundry)
rougir	to blush
bondir	to bounce / leap (also: rebondir)
réussir	to succeed (to pass an exam)
choisir	to choose
saisir	to grab
amollir	to soften

More will appear later in the book!

Exercice 48 - a

Copiez et complétez:
1. Je (amollir).
2. Nous (rougir).
3. Tu ne (grandir) pas.
4. On (élargir) la Rue des Saules.
5. Ils (réussir) tous leurs examens.

Exercice 48 - b

Employez les verbes Saisir; Choisir; Blanchir; Grossir; Bondir pour faire cinq petites phrases en français, puis traduisez vos phrases en anglais.

49. Recevoir   to receive

reçois	recevons
reçois	recevez
reçoit	reçoivent

Past participle:	reçu
Passé Composé:	J'ai reçu (etc.)

There are a few verbs which go like Recevoir:

apercevoir   to spot / notice / see
décevoir   to disappoint

Their past participles are: aperçu; déçu

« Déçu » is often used as an Adjective - disappointed.

Exercice 49 - a

Exprimez en français:
1. She receives.
2. I notice.
3. We (use: On) received.
4. They didn't notice the car.
5. Are you disappointed?

Exercice 49 - b

Inventez cinq phrases pour montrer (to show) les usages différents des verbes: recevoir; décevoir; apercevoir. Ecrivez au moins une question et une phrase au négatif.

50. The « Pas DE » Rule

After the word PAS, and other Negatives,

du, de la, de l', and des

...become DE:

J'ai des Bics rouges, mais je n'ai pas de stylos verts.
(I've got red biros, but I haven't got any green pens).

This is an important rule, which works for negative words other than PAS:

Tu n'as JAMAIS d'argent.	You never have any money.
Ici on ne voit PLUS de touristes, malheureusement.	You don't see tourists here any more, unfortunately.

Exercice 50 - a

Ecrivez au Négatif; utilisez le mot négatif indiqué:
1. Il a des disques de rap. (pas)
2. Nous regardons des films à la télé. (jamais)
3. Judith mange de la viande. (plus)
4. J'ai du lait écrémé (skimmed), madame. (pas)
5. On voit de l'eau par terre. (pas)

Exercice 50 - b

Ecrivez cinq phrases du même type que les phrases ci-dessus, et traduisez-les en anglais.

51. Quel / Quelle   Quels / Quelles   –   Which ?

a)   Masculine Singular: Quel ...?   M. Plural: Quels ...?
     Feminine Singular :   Quelle..?   F. Plural: Quelles..?

Quel ordinateur as-tu à la maison? Tu utilises quel logiciel?
(Which computer do you have at home? Which software do you use?).

Exercice 51 - a

Mettez la forme correcte de « Quel » devant chacun de ces mots. Ajoutez un point d'interrogation (?) après.
1. ballon (m)
2. calculatrice (f)
3. baladeurs (m)   [un baladeur = personal stereo]
4. cassette
5. caméras (f)

Exercice 51 - b

Exprimez en français:
1. Which spoon? [spoon = la cuiller]
2. Which windows?
3. Which glue-stick?   [glue-stick = le bâton-colle]
4. Which envelopes?   [f]
5. Which jeans?   [le jean]

b)   The words for 'Which?' are also used to say: 'What a ...!'
    Quelle journée! (What a day!) Quel beau temps! (What lovely weather!)

Note that French leaves out the word for 'a' in expressions like 'What a day!'

Quel toupet! (A polite expression for 'What a nerve!'!)

52. Le Passé Composé: Verbes Réguliers en -RE

J'ai rendu mes devoirs de maths ce matin en classe.
(I handed in my maths prep this morning in the lesson).

The same system is used as explained in 45 above, but note that the Past
Participles end in -u.

j'ai rendu	I gave back / handed in (etc.)
tu as vendu	you sold
il a attendu	he waited
elle a entendu	she heard
on a confondu	one has confused / mixed up (etc.)
nous avons répondu	we have answered
vous avez perdu	you lost
ils ont fondu	they melted (something)
elles ont rompu	they broke (off)

As with -ER Verbs, a part of Avoir is followed by a Past Participle.

Exercice 52 - a

Take five of the examples above (e.g. il a attendu), and say from which verb it
comes. E.g. il a attendu > Attendre, to wait.

Exercice 52 - b

Give another way of saying the examples above in English, e.g: tu as vendu is translated as 'you sold', but it also means 'you have sold'.

53. Croire   to believe

crois	croyons
crois	croyez
croit	croient

Past Participle: cru.   J'ai cru - I believed, I have believed.

54. Courir to run

cours	courons
cours	courez
court	courent

Past Participle: couru

BY THE WAY

** Are you beginning to notice how often the first 3 parts of Irregular Verbs end in S - S - T ?

Watch out for other useful patterns like this, which help to reduce timewasting when you learn something new!   **

---

55. Le Passé Composé.   Verbes Réguliers en -IR
(See 45 and 52 if you need to).

On a rempli les carafes d'eau fraîche. (They filled the jugs with cool water).
The same system as in 45 and 52 as above, but the Past Participles end in -i.

Exercice 55 - a

Donnez les Participes Passés des Verbes suivants:
1. remplir
2. punir
3. grandir
4. grossir
5. saisir
6. choisir
7. bondir
8. réussir
9. rougir
10. amollir

Exercice 55 - b

Traduisez en français:
1. She has grown!
2. It bounced (Use « il » for 'it').
3. They (f) grabbed.
4. He blushed.
5. The butter softened the beans. (les haricots).

Exercice 55 - c

Ecrivez cinq phrases au Passé Composé avec les Verbes ci-dessus, puis traduisez-les en anglais.

56. Past Participles of Irregular Verbs already included.

avoir	eu (had)	faire	fait	(done)
être	été(been)	falloir	fallu	(been necessary)
pouvoir	pu (been able)	vouloir	voulu	(wanted)
dire	dit (said)	lire	lu	(read)
prendre	pris (taken)	mettre	mis	(put)
tenir	tenu(held)	voir	vu	(seen)

savoir	su(known)	devoir	dû (had to)
boire	bu(drunk)	recevoir	reçu (received)
apercevoir	aperçu (noticed)	décevoir	déçu (disappointed)
croire	cru (believed)	courir	couru (run)

When you want to express these Verbs in the Passé Composé, use the right part of Avoir with the appropriate Past Participle (Participe Passé):

Elle a aperçu.   She noticed / She has noticed

57. Questions and Negatives in the Passé Composé

As-tu lu mon livre?   -   Non, je n'ai pas pu.
(Have you read my book? -   No, I haven't been able to).

As can be seen, the Participe Passé comes last in each Verb expression.

ALL THE CHANGING IS DONE TO AVOIR, then the Participe Passé is added.

Question Version of Avoir:

ai-je .....?	avons-nous...?
as-tu ....?	avez-vous.....?
a-t-il ....?	ont-ils...........?
a-t-elle .?	ont-elles........?
a-t-on ..?	

Negative Version of Avoir:
Je n'ai pas
Tu n'as pas   ... etc.

To make a Question that is Negative in the Passé Composé:

N'avez-vous pas trouvé les petites tasses?
(Haven't you found / Didn't you find ...?)

...all you do is take the whole Question form of Avoir and put Ne and Pas at each end:

Vous avez   > Avez-vous   > N' (avez-vous) pas...
...and, once again, add your Participe Passé to the end:

N'avez-vous pas trouvé?

When there are Direct Object Pronouns in PC Questions and PC Negative Questions, they go before the Avoir part, but this is fully explained in 106 below.

Exercice 57 - a

Ecrivez à l'Interrogatif (Rewrite these sentences as questions):
1.   On a oublié les serviettes.
2.   Tu as apporté de l'essuie-tout.
3.   Vous avez vu mon oncle.
4.   Elles n'ont pas pris les bics bleus.
5.   On n'a pas dit bonjour à Madame Laidet.

Exercice 57 - b

Ecrivez cinq petites phrases au Passé Composé et réécrivez-les au Négatif.

58. Calendar: Days and Months

Le quatorze juillet on fête la Prise de la Bastille.
(On July 14, we celebrate the Taking of the Bastille).

You probably know the days and months. If not, LEARN them:

a) *Les Jours de la Semaine* (In order, starting with Monday):
 lundi   mardi   mercredi   jeudi   vendredi   samedi   dimanche

b) *Les Mois de l'Année:*
 janvier   février   mars   avril   mai   juin   juillet   août   septembre
 octobre   novembre   décembre

Dates are written: le 1er août   (1er - first - is the only date
                                          written as an ordinal number).
                      le 19 mai   (All dates except 1st are written
                                          this way).

Watch out for: le 11   (le onze - you'd expect *l'onze*).

You may write a date with the number in full (like the first example) but it is not usual.

c) From... to...

La pâtisserie sera fermée du 21 août au 10 septembre.
The pâtisserie will be closed from the 21st August to the 10th September).
La liste des gagnants sera disponible à partir du 15 mai.
(The list of winners will be available from the 15th May).

Exercice 58

Study the examples above and write:
a) Ten examples of dates in French, using different numbers and months each time;
b) Five sentences using either « du... au... » or « à partir du... », as in c) above.

59. Revision of Faire and Weather Expressions, Present, Past and Future.

Faire   to do, to make

fais   faisons
fais   faites
fait   font

Irreg. Future stem: fer-
Past Participle: fait

Remember :   « Il fait beau » etc. Faire is used in many Weather Expressions.

THINK about it: Weather is something you hardly ever ask about in the present tense (What is the weather like?) unless you're on the phone. Most other uses are, in practice, generally past or future.

Il a fait très beau pendant plusieurs jours puis il a plu.
(It was lovely for several days then it rained).
Demain il fera assez chaud sur les régions du centre et de l'ouest...
(Tomorrow it'll be quite warm in central and western parts...).
Consider the same example in the 3 tenses you know:

Il fait froid   Il fera froid   Il a fait froid

Exercice 59 - a

All you need to complete the picture (for the moment!) are the future and past of the other weather verbs. To get thinking, here are the raw materials; you can work the rest out for yourself:

In the columns below are each Verb, its Future Stem and its Past Participle. The first set is done for you:

Verbe	Racine du futur	Participe Passé
faire	fer-	fait
> il fait froid	> il fera froid	> il a fait froid
pleuvoir (il pleut)	pleuvr-	plu
neiger	neiger-	neigé
geler (to freeze)	gèler-	gelé
être*	ser-	été

* Etre is used with Adjectives to describe the weather, e.g:

pluvieux (rainy); nuageux (cloudy); couvert (overcast); triste (gloomy).

Exercice 59 - b

Traduisez en anglais vos exemples de l'exercice 59 - a.

60. Avoir Expresions (Those not using 'to have' in English).

Tiens, j'ai chaud! Allons à la piscine!
(I'm hot! Let's go swimming).

You'll already know « J'ai dix ans » (I have ten years) for 'I'm ten'.

Revise or learn:

avoir chaud	to be hot (person)	avoir faim	to be hungry
avoir soif	to be thirsty	avoir raison	to be right
avoir tort	to be wrong	avoir l'air...	to seem...
avoir sommeil	to be sleepy	avoir honte	to be ashamed
avoir besoin (de)	to need	avoir envie (de)	to really want
avoir peur	to be afraid	avoir la pêche	to feel on top of the world

If necessary, revise Avoir (25), not forgetting the Futur (aur-) or the Participe Passé (eu).

When describing things, with the appropriate words, use être, not avoir; when expressing weather, use faire or other weather words.

L'eau de la piscine est froide, et quand il fait beau et j'ai chaud j'aime me baigner.

(The swimming-pool water is cold, and when it's fine and I'm hot, I like to go for a swim.)

Exercice 60 - a

Exprimez en français:
1. It's cold (refering to the weather).
2. It's cold (refering to la table).
3. She's sleepy.
4. They need their pens and exercise books.
5. I really feel great today!

Exercice 60 - b

Traduisez en français: (Refer to 57 or any other sections as necessary).
1. Are you hungry?
2. Isn't he ashamed?
3. She wasn't thirsty.
4. We were afraid!
5. You're right, they didn't seem happy.

61. Numbers

Les nombres - numbers in general; Les chiffres - figures / statistics
Les numéros - individual numbers (e.g. Question numbers, house numbers).

You may know the spellings of all the numbers. If not, check them in your normal textbook or ask your teacher. They are not listed here.

Get used to French numbers QUICKLY! One way is to practise saying them while looking at figures.

Exercice 61 - a

Lisez, le plus vite possible, ces numéros:

2	5	7	3	15	23	46	32	21	12	16	18	37
53	35	29	19	4	0	59	41	54	47	22	61	13
26	11	20	25	8	36	64	69	1	28			

Exercice 61 - b

The awkward ones are from 70 to 80, and from 90 to 99. Count several times without stopping, from 70 (soixante-dix) to 99 (quatre-vingt-dix-neuf).

French telephone numbers are set out in pairs: 44.56.87.02 and are read out as such (quarante-quatre, cinquante-six...) so it is useful to practise hearing them and writing them down, and reading them out yourself.

07 (etc.) is said: 'zéro sept'.

Exercice 61 - c

Avec votre partenaire, inventez et lisez une liste de cinq numéros de téléphone. Il / elle doit les écrire sans regarder ce que vous lisez.

62. Qui/Que   Relative Pronouns (referring to previous words).

Qui est-ce?   Ah, c'est l'homme qui vend les t-shirts que j'aime.
(Who's that? Oh, it's the man who sells the t-shirts which I like)

Qui means: Who   / Which   / That
Que means: Who(m)   / Which   / That

and, of course, they also have their Question-word meanings (Qui = Who?; Que = What?)

Read through these examples, and try to get used to them:

Le pantalon que tu aimes est dans l'armoire.
(The trousers which you like are in the wardrobe).
Les socquettes que Natalie choisit sont blanches.
(The ankle socks which Natalie chooses are white).
L'autobus qui va au centre-ville est le vingt-sept.
(The bus which goes to the town centre is the No. 27)

In the 3rd example, « Qui » is used, because the word it refers to is L'autobus, which is a SUBJECT word (i.e. l'autobus does the action of the verb « va »).

In the other two, « Que » is used, because the words it refers to are OBJECT words (the liking and choosing are done to the trousers and socks).

TIP   An even easier way to ensure you are right in this sort of case, is to see if the very next word after Qui/Que is a VERB. If it is, you use QUI.

Finally, Que is shortened to Qu' before a vowel. Qui is never shortened.

Exercice 62 - a

Remplissez les trous:
1. Voici l'album _____ contient toutes les photos de ma famille.
2. Les jeux électroniques _____ elle cherche ne sont plus là.
3. Le couteau _____ j'ai trouvé dans le tiroir est sale.
4. Qu'est-ce _____ tu veux faire cet après-midi?
5. Qu'est-ce _____ fait ce bruit agaçant? (irritating)

Exercice 62 - b

Traduisez l'exercice 62 - a en anglais.
One further word of warning:

In English, 'who', 'which' and 'that' may sometimes be left out altogether, so be very careful to notice when Qui or Que should appear in French. They cannot be left out at all in French. The title of the song 'The Man I Love' would have to be 'L'homme QUE j'aime' in French!

63. Celui / Celle   Ceux / Celles
The one (m/f)   The ones (m/f)   etc.

Celle que j'ai voulu essayer n'est plus là.
(The one which I wanted to try on isn't there any more).

These are very simple and just need practice. They are also used to point things out, followed by -ci or -là:

Lequel (see 64 below) voulez-vous? (Which one do you want?)
- Celui-là, s'il vous plaît. (That one, please)

There are more than one way of expressing these words in English:

Celles-ci sont très belles.	These are really nice.
	These ones are really nice.

Which to use depends on the Noun you are refering to. (m/f; s/pl):

La voiture qu'il va acheter	>	Celle qu'il va acheter (The one he's going to buy)
Les pâtes qu'on va manger	>	Celles qu'on va manger (The ones we're going to eat)
L'homme à la casquette bleue	>	Celui à la casquette bleue (The one with the blue cap)
Les feux du centre-ville	>	Ceux du centre-ville (The ones in the town centre)

The phrase « Celui-là » / « Celle-là » is also used in literature to refer to the 'last person mentioned', rather like 'the latter' in English.

Exercice 63 - a

Copiez, en traduisant les mots anglais en français:
1. The ones (f) que tu veux sont trop chères.
2. The one (m) que j'ai vu hier - c'est lui!
3. Papa n'a pas goûté (tasted) those (f) de la nouvelle pâtisserie.
4. Voulez-vous this one (m) ou that one (m)?
5. One of those (m) s'il vous plaît.

Exercice 63 - b

Ecrivez dix exemples, de la façon suivante (in the following way):

l'ordinateur - m/s - celui   celui-ci ; celui-là

... using any ten nouns of your choice, with as much variety as possible.

64. Revision of Question Words and use of Est-ce que...?

a)

Que ... ?	What ... ?
Qui ... ?	Who ... ?
Pourquoi ... ?	Why ... ?
Quand ... ?	When ... ?
Comment ... ?	How ... ?
Où ... ?	Where ... ?
Combien (de) ... ?	How many ... or How much ... ?
Tous les combien ... ?	How often ... ?
Quel (etc.) ... ?	Which ... ?

Apart from the ones above, LEARN the following. *It* is a pronoun, since it is used so you don't have to repeat the noun:

It means 'Which one?' or 'Which ones?' depending on whether it is singular or plural, and you form it simply by adding the words for 'Which?' to the words for 'The':

lequel?　　　　laquelle?　　　　lesquels?　　lesquelles?

b)　　Est-ce que ... ?

Creates a question out of what follows it:

Il a fait de l'orage.　　　　It was stormy.
Est-ce qu'il a fait de l'orage?　Was it stormy?

Est-ce que is an alternative to other question forms. What follows it MUST be a statement, because *Est-ce que* makes it into a question.
You can put other question words BEFORE Est-ce que:

Quand est-ce que tu pars?　　When are you leaving?

Exercice 64.

Say whether the following questions are correct French or not; if they aren't, say why not:

1. Est-ce qu'il arrive à midi? 2. Combien de tomates veut-elle?
3. Est-ce que voulez-vous celui-ci? 4. Est-ce que lequel tu mets?
5. Où est-ce qu'on va aller?

65. **Further Negatives.**

Pourquoi aller au Saxo? Il n'y a jamais plus personne!
(Why go to the Saxo Club? There's never anyone there nymore!).

See 2 and 27 above to check on the basic rule.

ne...jamais - never (not ever)   ne...personne - no-one (not anyone)
ne...plus - no more (not anymore, no longer, not any longer)
ne...ni...ni - neither ... nor   ne...point - not at all

You may also come across:

ne...nulle part - nowhere (not anywhere)
ne...aucun(e) - no (followed by a noun -e.g. Il n'y a aucun problème)
ne...guère   - hardly

...and an expression with 'ne' that is not really negative:

ne...que - only

ATTENTION!
1. « Rien », « Ni... ni », « Jamais », « Aucun(e) » and « Personne » can start
sentences, so they may also come *before* « ne » and the verb:
Personne n'arrive avant dix heures - Nobody arrives before ten o'clock.

2. In the Passé Composé, MOST Negatives come before the Participe Passé:

Je n'ai rien fait. Il n'a jamais triché (He's never cheated).

Personne comes after the Participe Passé:

On n'a vu personne.

3. Any number of negatives may be used, but with each Verb, « ne » is only said
once (See the first example at the beginning of 65).

French: *Towards GCSE*

Exercice 65 - a

Complétez avec le Negatif qu'il faut:
1. Jean-Jacques a regardé le match.   (not)
2. Tu as rencontré mes parents?(never)
3. On va au Club Saxo.   (no more) .
4. Nous emmenons (bring) Jules et* Xavier.(neither...nor)   *Attention!
5. Je suis désolée, j'ai celles-ci. (only)
(Make sure you've made the right verb negative in No. 5. There are 2!)

Don't forget that, after a Negative, Du / De la / De l' / Des all have to become
DE:

On ne voit guère de 2 CV de nos jours.
(You hardly see any 2 CVs these days).

With ni..ni, « de » is often left out:

Les sans-abri n'ont ni domicile ni emploi...
(The 'homeless' have neither a home nor a job).

66. Adverbs: Regular formation and Irregulars.

« Je suis la première de la classe,» a-t-elle dit fièrement.
(I'm at the top of the class, she said proudly).

a) Adverbs normally end in -ment, rather like -ly in English, this endinbeing
added onto the Adjective:

vrai (true)   >   vraiment (truly, really)

b)   A vowel is needed before the -ment ending, so many Adjectives
have to be made Feminine (to give a final -e) before -ment is added:

lent (slow)   >   lentement (slowly)

This means that all the Irregular Feminines of Adjectives must be known! So do
check 21 above if necessary.

Voici quelques exemples:

Adjectif	Adjectif au Féminin	Adverbe
doux	douce	doucement
actif	active	activement
nouveau	nouvelle	nouvellement

c) Adjectives with the ending -ent or -ant change it to: -emment or -amment:

évident	>	évidemment (obvious/ly)
bruyant	>	bruyamment (noisy > noisily)

d) Some Adverbs are totally irregular and must be learnt specially:

bon	>	bien
mauvais	>	mal
gentil	>	gentiment
précis	>	précisément (é, not e)
rapide	>	vite (quickly)/rapidement

Other adverbs will appear in the book. See if you can tell which categories they fall into.

67. Comparison of Adjectives and Adverbs.

Jean est plus adroit que Marcel.
(Jean is more skilful than Marcel).

+	plus	='more'; the -er ending of 'taller' etc. is done this way also.
−	moins	='less'
=	aussi	='as ... as'
..	que	= than (or the 2nd 'as' of 'as ... as')

Tu es aussi grand que moi?   Ah non, je suis un peu plus grand que toi.
(Are you as tall as me?   Ah no, I'm a bit taller than you.)

The same rule applies to Adverbs, except that Adjectives must still agree with the noun they describe, whereas Adverbs do not change.

Ma voiture est moins belle que la Renault, mais elle roule plus vite.
(My car is less beautiful than the Renault, but it goes faster.)

Exercice 67 - a

Copiez et complétez, selon le symbole à côté de chaque phrase:
1. Sophie est ....habile ....Claire.   (+)
2. Arthur travaille.........dur.........Raymond.   (−)
3. La Twingo est ....bruyante............la R5.   (=)
4. La plage est..........loin.........le camping.   (+)
5. Les parents sont..........agaçants ....les petits frères.(YOU decide!)

Exercice 67 - b

Inventez cinq phrases de comparaison qui emploient les mots suivants:
1. les soeurs / embêtant (annoying) / les animaux.
2. ma mobylette / rapidement / ta bicyclette.
3. les campings en ville / poussiéreux (dusty) / les campings à la plage.
4. les robochefs (food processors) / efficace (effective) / les fouets.
5. Charles / fort en maths / Marie.

THINK! Have you checked that your Adjective agrees with its noun, and that your Adverb has no agreement? You needed a verb for each of these five sentences: did you put one in? Verbs you could have used are: être, rouler, crier; but they aren't the only possibilities.

Irregular Comparatives of Adjectives and Adverbs:

Bon	>	Meilleur	(Good	> Better)
Bien	>	Mieux	(Well	> Better)
Mauvais	>	Pire	(Bad	> Worse)
Mal	>	Pis	(Badly	> Worse)

(NOTE: French sometimes prefers 'moins bien' to the 'worse' Adverbs).

68. Superlative of Adjectives and Adverbs.

Agnan est le plus fort de la classe en calcul. (Agnan's the best in the form at maths)

Adjectives: Just add *le, la* or *les* to the comparative, but leave off '*que*':

L'écriture de Caroline est la meilleure de la classe.

N.B. We use 'la' and make meilleure fem. to agree with 'écriture'.

Adverbs: Just put *le* (only) before the comparative, leaving off '*que*':

Caroline écrit le mieux.

Finally, to say 'in' (the best *in* the world, etc.), use '*de*':

La plus haute du monde   The highest in the world.
Le moins vite de la classe The least quickly in the class.

Exercice 68

Traduisez en français:
1. She types (to type = taper) the fastest.
2. It's papa who drives the slowest.
3. Food processors are the most effective.
4. English cartoons (les BD) are the funniest (funny = rigolo).
5. I watch them the most often.

69. Si: 'If' and 'Yes' in <u>disagreement.</u>

Tu n'aimes pas les pâtes?   Si, surtout à la sauce napolitaine!
You don't like pasta?   Yes I do, especially in Napolitan sauce!

Alors, tu les aimes si elles sont cuisinées à l'italienne?   Oui, c'est ça.
So, you like it if it's cooked the italian way?   Yes, that's right.

Exercice 69.

If you wanted to answer 'yes' to all these questions, you would answer 'oui' sometimes, but 'si' if the question was negative. How would you answer 'yes' to these questions?:

1. Tu aimes les haricots verts?
2. Vous n'allez pas passer nous dire bonjour?
3. On va à la piscine?
4. Ton père ne va pas aller à la pêche aujourd'hui?
5. Tu veux du pain?

70. Ecrire to write; Décrire to describe

écris	écrivons
écris	écrivez
écrit	écrivent

Participe passé: écrit
Racine du futur: écrir-

Décrire follows exactly the same pattern.

The Nouns associated with these verbs are a little different:

l'écriture   handwriting;   la description   description.

Another associated Verb is: s'inscrire   to 'sign up' for something.

71. Connaître to know (a person or place)

connais	connaissons
connais	connaissez
connaît	connaissent

Participe passé: connu
Racine du futur: connaîtr-

paraître, to seem or appear; and disparaître, to disappear, follow the same pattern.

Associated words: la connaissance   knowledge / consciousness
                            reconnaissant   grateful
                            la disparition   disappearance (or: death)
(Many words from 'disparaître' are used in French as euphemisms for death!)

Paraître: to appear, also means 'to appear on sale for the first time'.
Le livre vient de paraître   -   The book's 'just out'.

72. Verbs normally followed by Infinitives.

Je voudrais acheter ce livre. (I'd like <u>to buy</u> this book).

Whereas some Verbs are followed by a Preposition (à or de) and then an Infinitive, there are a few which have just an Infinitive after them:

aimer	
aller	
désirer	*to want to*
devoir	
espérer	*to hope to*
faire	*to have something done*
falloir	
laisser	*to allow*
oser	*to dare*
pouvoir	
vouloir	(*including*: je voudrais, *etc.*)
préférer	(*also*: aimer mieux, *to prefer*)
savoir	*to know how to*
sembler	*to seem (to be ...ing)*
venir	

Some are less obvious:

écouter	J'écoute chanter les oiseaux - *I listen to the birds sing.*
entendre	On entend clapoter l'eau - *You hear the water lapping.*

Exercice 72 - a

Exprimez en français:

1. She knows how to windsurf (to windsurf/ use a sailboard = faire de la planche à voile).
2. How dare you say that!
3. You (use: « on ») can eat here at midnight, if you want.
4. Don't you know how to swim? - Yes!
5. I prefer to go on foot.

Exercice 72 - b

Ecrivez cinq phrases avec des verbes suivis d'Infinitifs.

73. Le Passé Composé - Verbs using Etre instead of Avoir.

Je suis passé dire bonjour à Jérôme, puis on est allé jouer au volley.
(I dropped by to say hello to Jérôme, then we went to play volleyball).

1.   MEMORISE: GOING-Verbs GO with ETRE!

There are so few exceptions to this that it is an excellent guideline.

It means that nearly all Verbs that have a sense of 'going' in their meaning form their Passé Composé with Etre, not Avoir.

NOTE also that the Participe Passé must agree (like an Adjective) with the Subject (je, tu etc.):

> je suis monté(e)   I went upstairs / I went up (the road), etc.
> tu es monté(e)
> il est monté
> elle est montée
> on est monté
> nous sommes monté(e)s
> vous êtes monté(e)(s) (« vous » can be Singular or Plural)
> ils sont montés
> elles sont montées

The principal Verbs going with Etre are:

aller	to go
arriver	to arrive
descendre	to go down / downstairs, etc.
entrer	to go / come in / to enter
partir	to go away / to set off
sortir	to go out
rester	to stay
retourner	to return / to turn back
tomber	to fall
venir	to come
revenir	to come back

There are also the Verbs meaning to come into the world and to go out of it!

naître	to be born
mourir	to die (these two are given in full in 89 below).

Add to these a couple of important Verbs associated with a few of the above:

redescendre	to go back down
rentrer	to go back in
ressortir	to go back out
repartir	to go away again, to set off again

2.   All REFLEXIVE Verbs go with Etre.

This rule is practically unique in French, as there are NO EXCEPTIONS!

Exemple: Elles se sont précipitées à la sortie de secours.
               (They rushed to the fire-exit).

Reflexive Verbs are revised more fully in 74 below.
Exercises for 73 and 74 are together below, in 74.

74. Revision of Reflexive Verbs

Il se vante devant ses copains parce qu'il se croit supérieur.
(He boasts in front of his friends because he thinks himself to be superior).

As you know, some French Reflexive Verbs are not reflexive in English.

s'en aller	to go (off / away)
s'arrêter	to stop (oneself, not something else)
se dépêcher	to hurry
se précipiter	to rush
se souvenir (de)	to remember
se rappeler	to recall
se taire	to stop talking (Remember Tais-toi! - Be quiet! ?)
s'approcher de	to go up to (to get nearer to)
se vanter	to boast
s'imaginer	to imagine

These are not the only ones! Simply remember, as you come across Verbs that are reflexive in one language but not the other, to apply all the right rules.

Les Verbes Réfléchis au Présent:

je me lave	nous nous lavons
tu te laves	vous vous lavez
il se lave	ils se lavent
elle se lave	elles se lavent
on se lave	

Les Verbes Réfléchis à l'Infinitif:

ATTENTION! In the INFINITIVE, the Reflexive Pronoun (me, te, etc.) MUST be the right one for the Person:

Je veux ME laver. -   I want to wash MYSELF

Any other reflexive pronoun here would make nonsense of the phrase.

Les Verbes Réfléchis au Passé Composé:

Note the ORDER: Person + Refl. Pronoun + Part of ETRE + Participe Passé:

Elle   s'   est   arrêtée

Learn this short passage and try to say it without checking back:

Je me suis levé(e), je me suis lavé(e), je me suis habillé(e), je me suis brossé(e) les cheveux, et je suis descendu(e) à la cuisine, où j'ai pris le petit déjeuner.

In this Passé Composé passage, you have 4 reflexives, 1 être-verb and 1 verb going with avoir.

Exercice 73/74 - a

Ecrivez le passage ci-dessus (above):
1.   ...pour « elle »;
2.   ...pour « nous »;
3.   ...pour « on »;

Exercice 73/74 - b

Go back to 73 and write five Passé Composé Etre-verb expressions, giving the meaning of each one.

Exemple: Elles sont redescendues - They (f) went back downstairs.

Now see 74 and write five Passé Composé Reflexive Verb expressions, giving the meanings.

Exemple: On s'est précipité   -   We rushed.

Finally, remember that ANY verb may be made reflexive (and follow all the above rules) as long as it makes sense:

J'ai trouvé le cinéma   -   I found the cinema.
Je me suis trouvé devant le cinéma   -   I found myself outside the cinema.

BY THE WAY

In the Passé Composé, any verb that has a Direct Object MUST go with AVOIR. This means that some verbs express different things with Avoir in the P.C. than with Etre:

Je suis sorti	–	I went out.
J'ai sorti mon carnet	–	I took out my notebook.

---

75. Pendant   and   Pendant Que

Pendant le trajet, j'ai lu un roman entier.
(During the journey, I read a whole novel).

Je vais écrire une lettre pendant qu'il lit.
(I'm going to write a letter while he reads).

Pendant	means	DURING
Pendant que	means	WHILE

Try not to mix them up! There is no other mystery about them.

76. Etre sur le Point de + Infinitif

David et Jo sont sur le point d'aller à la pêche aux bulots.
(David and Jo are about to go whelk-fishing).

Etre sur le point de... = To be about to...

Simply use Etre as you would normally, add « sur le point de » and the appropriate Infinitive.

Exercice 76 - a

Traduisez en français:
1.   She's about to listen to her walkman.
2.   Nadia's about to nip off (to nip off = filer).

3.   They're about to leave.
4.   Pierre and Antoine are about to arrive.
5.   Are you about to eat?

Exercice 76 - b

Pensez à cinq exemples d' être sur le point de...

77. Etre en Train de + Infinitif

L'animatrice est en train d'accueillir un *nouveau* groupe.
(The organiser is [in the process of] welcoming a new group).

This is another expression using Etre (see 76):
Notice that it means to be 'in the process of' doing something, but in English you can express it different ways:

Il est en train de faire la cuisine.   He's in the process of cooking.
                                                    He's cooking.
                                                    He's just cooking.

You simply have to decide if you need en train de to make it absolutely clear what is meant.

Exercice 77 - a

Exprimez en anglais:
1.   On est en train de ranger nos chambres.
2.   Qu'est-ce que tu es en train de faire?
3.   Le papa de Georges est en train d'écrire un roman.

Exercice 77 - b
Pensez à deux exemples en anglais, d'être en train de...', puis traduisez-les en français.

78. C'est > C'était > Ce sera > Ç'a été

C'était affreux hier, mais ce sera meilleur demain.
(It was awful yesterday, but it'll be better tomorrow).

C'est (it is) is part of être, so to say 'It was' or 'It will be',
you use other tenses of être with « ce » ('it'):

Présent	:	C'est
Futur	:	Ce sera (It will be)
P. Composé	:	Ç'a été (It has been / It was)

Then there is the first expression you probably learnt using the Imparfait (Imperfect Tense):

Imparfait	:	C'était (It was)

C'était is usually used descriptively.

There is more on the Imparfait in 92 below.

Exercice 78

Exprimez en français:
1. It's a little difficult.
2. It was amazing (amazing - sensass) [descriptive].
3. It'll be good (bien) if you come by to say hello.
4. It's been a real pleasure.
5. It was my brother on the phone (on the = au).

C'est etc. au Négatif:

Remember that *c'est* is short for ce + est, so, before « ne », c' becomes ce again:

C'est à toi? (Is it yours?) - Non, ce n'est pas à moi.
Ce n'était pas juste (It wasn't fair).

79. Depuis + Present Tense (Since / For)

Ils sont là depuis trois heures. (They've been there for three hours).

Depuis really means since, so the example really means:

They are there since three hours.

Ask yourself: Are they *still* there? If so, the Verb MUST be present tense. More generally, if the action of the verb is still happening, the Verb is Present.

(They have been there for three hours and still are).

Exercice 79 - a

Say in which of these sentences you would need to use Depuis + Present:
1. She's been reading for twenty minutes.
2. I've been waiting for hours.
3. They sat there for about ten minutes.
4. The Thompsons are going to France for three weeks.
5. They've lived in the USA for a year.

Exercice 79 - b

Translate the sentences you have selected in Exercice 79 - a into French.

80. Venir de + Infinitif (To have just...)

Allô! Maman? On vient d'arriver! (Hello! Mum? We've just got here!).

Revise Venir in the Present Tense (31).

Venir is used with any Infinitive to mean to have just (done).

In French, if you 'come from eating', it means that eating was the last thing you did, just now.

Je viens de manger - (I come from eating) - I have just eaten.

Exercice 80 - a

Exprimez en français:
1. They've just gone inside the museum.
2. She's just come out of the pharmacy.
3. I've just noticed the date (to notice = remarquer).
4. Philippe's just been on the t.v! (to be on t.v.= passer à la télé).
5. I'm sorry, they've just left.

Exercice 80 - b

Ecrivez en français cinq phrases avec Venir de + Infinitif. Traduisez vos phrases en anglais.

81. Conduire to drive - and similar Verbs

conduis	conduisons
conduis	conduisez
conduit	conduisent

Participe Passé: conduit (Goes with Avoir in the Passé Composé)
Racine du Futur: conduir-

Verbs following the same pattern as Conduire include:

construire	to construct / build
traduire	to translate
détruire	to destroy
construire	to construct / build
réduire	to reduce

There are quite a few Nouns associated with these Verbs:

traduire	>	la traduction (translation)
détruire	>	la destruction

What do you think are the Nouns from réduire and construire?
What do they mean?

82. Se Promener and Faire une Promenade –
A Case for Clear Thinking!

Nous nous sommes promenés au bord du lac.   (We walked by the lake).

Nous avons fait une promenade au bord du lac. (We went for a walk by the lake).

Of course, there is hardly any difference between these expressions, but for that reason alone you have to be all the more aware which Verb is being used in each case, so you apply the right rules.

1. Se promener - a Reflexive Verb.   2. Faire.

In the second sentence, what sort of word is *une promenade* ?

It is a Noun, (an outing, a walk, etc.) - nothing like the Verb.

There are many expressions using Faire, which use different verbs in English. Make sure you learn these when they appear in your coursebook.

83. More Irregular Adjective Feminines

a)   Adjectives ending in -eux in the Masculine > -euse in the Feminine.

    silencieux   >   silencieuse   -silent
    délicieux   >   délicieuse   -delicious

b)   Adjectives ending in -er in the Masculine > -ère in the Feminine.

    premier   >   première   -first
    dernier   >   dernière   -last

Exercice 83

Exprimez en français:
1. This peach is delicious.
2. She arrived first (put 'the' before 'first').
3. Last week, it rained.
4. Sophie-Marie is very proud of her house.
5. The streets are silent.

84. Irregular Past Participles Revisited

We need to bring these up to date to include the Verbs that have been introduced since the last list (56 above), even though they can be worked out from their model Verb's pattern:

Verbe	Participe Passé	P.Composé	
décrire	décrit	j'ai décrit	I have described
paraître	paru	il a paru	it seemed
venir	venu	je suis venu	I have come
construire	construit	j'ai construit	I have built
détruire	détruit	j'ai détruit	I have destroyed

To these, we will complete the picture (for this part of the book) by adding the rest of the Past Participles of Irregular Verbs which will appear.

naître	né	je suis né	I was born
mourir	mort	il est mort	he has died
couvrir	couvert	j'ai couvert	I have covered
découvrir	découvert	j'ai découvert	I've discovered
offrir	offert	j'ai offert	I've offered/given
souffrir	souffert	j'ai souffert	I have suffered
rire	ri	j'ai ri	I laughed
sourire	souri	j'ai souri	I smiled
peindre	peint	j'ai peint	I've painted
joindre	joint	j'ai joint	I have joined
éteindre	éteint	j'ai éteint	I've turned of (the lights etc.)

85. Après avoir / Après être / Après s'être   + Participe Passé

Après avoir trouvé la lampe de poche, nous sommes descendus dans la cave. (Having found the torch, we went down into the cellar).

We use « Après AVOIR » in this case, because Trouver (to find) goes with Avoir in the Passé Composé.

		trouvé
	avoir	fini
Après	être	fait
	s'être	couché
		rentré

The Participes Passés in the right-hand column above are from Verbs either going with Avoir, or Etre, or they are Reflexive Verbs.

Exercice 85 - a

Re-read the example above (under the title), then re-arrange the elements of the substitution-table above to make 5 phrases.

Exemple: Après être sorti... = (After) Having gone out...
This one is correct because Sortir goes with être.

ATTENTION! Be careful to get Reflexives right: Just as with the Infinitive of a Reflexive Verb, you must put the correct Reflexive Pronoun:

	m'		
	t'		endormi
Après	s'	être	arrêté
	nous		levé
	vous		

...and remember to add -e or -s (or both) if appropriate, to the Participe Passé.

A few examples, for you to get used to this construction:

Après avoir vu Michel, elles sont allées à la poste.
Après être sorties, elles ont pris l'autobus.
Après avoir composté leur billet, elles se sont assises.
Après s'être assises, elles ont commencé à lire.

Concentrate on the parts before the comma; notice which Participes Passés have been made to agree: the ones with Etre, including the Reflexive.

Exercice 85 - b:

Traduisez les exemples ci-dessus (above) en anglais.

86. Etre-Verbs in the Passé Composé – A Reminder of Ending Agreement

Elles sont montées au premier étage, où elles se sont installées.
(They (f) went up to the first floor, where they settled in).

The endings of all Participes Passés of Verbs going with Etre (73) are made to agree with the Subject:

	Avoir + pp	:	Marie et Caroline ont voyagé par le train.
But	Etre + pp	:	Marie et Caroline sont arrivées en retard.

This is also true of ALL Reflexive Verbs (because they all go with Etre).

Verbe Réfléchi :   Marie et Caroline se sont installées.

87. Suffire   to be enough / to be sufficient

suffis	suffisons
suffis	suffisez
suffit	suffisent

Participe Passé: Suffi
Racine du Futur: Suffir-

Suffire has been included because of the frequent use of certain of its forms:

« Jean-Jacques! Ça suffit! » (Parent to child!)
« Ça suffira comme ça? » (Shop assistant when measuring out quantities -Will that be enough like that?)

88. En ...ant   and Irregular Present Participles.

En jouant au football il s'est cassé la cheville.
(Playing football, he broke his ankle).

Briefly, EN is used (to mean by / on / in / while   ...ing) with the Present Participle, when the second action is a result of the first, or is happening at the same time.

This includes intended results:

En réservant votre place d'avance, vous pourrez vous assurer d'une soirée inoubliable.
(By reserving your seat in advance, you'll be certain to have an unforgettable evening).

When the two actions are consecutive (one AFTER the other), and the sense of 'on / by / while / in' is not meant, EN is left out. (EN implies a clear connection between the first action and the second):

Oubliant la lettre, il est allé directement en ville.
(Forgetting the letter, he went straight into town).

ALL Present Participles end in -ant, and only a few Irregular Verbs have Irregular stems:

étant	(être)	being
sachant	(savoir)	knowing
ayant	(avoir)	having

The rest form the Pres. Part. from the NOUS - form of the Present Tense, taking off -ons and adding -ant:

Nous finiss**ons** > finiss**ant**   (finishing)

Exercice 88 - a

Formez les Participes Présents des Verbes suivants:
1. Aller   2.   Vendre   3. Faire   4. Réduire   5. Ecrire

Exercice 88 - b

Exprimez en français:
1. Forgetting the parcel, she went out.
2. Opening the door, he was able to see inside (use l'intérieur).
3. On arriving at her house, he rang the bell. (Verb: sonner)
4. Playing tennis, he broke his arm.
5. Writing to his mother, he thought of (à) his friends at home.

NOTE: Some Present Participle expressions in English are differently done in French:

Seeing is believing	:	Voir, c'est croire.
We love rollerskating	:	Nous adorons faire du patin à roulettes.

As you can see, these two are expressed by the Infinitive in French.

89. Naître to be born; Mourir to die

Naître:

nais	naissons
nais	naissez
naît	naissent

Participe Passé:	né
Racine du Futur:	naîtr-

Mourir:

meurs	mourons
meurs	mourez
meurt	meurent

Participe Passé:	mort
Racine du Futur:	mourr-

Both these Verbs go with Etre: Elle est née - She was born
                                 Ils sont morts - They have died

90. Autant: Autant que / Autant de

Il mange autant de pommes anglaises que de pommes françaises.
(He eats as many English apples as French apples).
Elle aime le jazz, mais pas autant que moi.
(She likes jazz, but not as much as me).

Autant means 'as much'; 'as many'. The difference between *autant que* and *autant de* is summarised briefly by the two examples above.

Exercice 90

Traduisez en anglais:
1. Il y a autant de garçons que de filles.
2. Le maire aime les Hollandais autant que les Anglais.
3. L'épicière vend autant de vin blanc que de vin rouge.

Maintenant, inventez deux phrases pour montrer la différence entre « autant que » et « autant de ».

91. Irregular Future Stems - A Word of Advice

Revise the Irregular Future stems in section 16, above. Then check through all the Irregular Verbs listed since then to see if any have Irregular Future stems.

You are going to need to be aware of them:

a) so you don't confuse them with the Imparfait (92);
b) for forming the Conditionnel (95).

92. L'Imparfait   (The Imperfect Tense)

Au moment où je suis entré, Daniel dessinait et Simone lisait son livre.
(At the moment I came in, Daniel was drawing and Simone was reading her book).

The Imparfait is another Past tense, like the Passé Composé. Knowing it enables you to express past events, and understand what you read or hear, much more completely than just knowing the Passé Composé.

Uses:		
	1. Setting the scene	(Description in the past: It was a fine day; there were no clouds, etc.).
	2. Was...ing / Were...ing	(Daniel was drawing; they were playing).
	3. Used to...	('Habits'-things done regularly- in the past: He used to play boules on Sundays; Marie's mum smoked in those days).

French: *Towards GCSE*

Formation:

a) Stem: The NOUS form of the Present Tense, without -ons:
   Nous faisons   >   fais-
b) Endings: -ais   -ions
            -ais   -iez
            -ait   -aient
c) Exceptions: Only ONE !!   Etre:

ALL Verbs have the same rules and same pattern of endings.
The STEM for être, however, is: ét- .

You have come across « ét- » before in the word « était »(was).

ATTENTION! 90 % of all accidents involving the Imparfait occur because people are thinking of English constructions, not French:

I was reading   J'étais lisant .   X   (Horribly wrong)
                    Je lisais.   (Correct).

So THINK about what you are trying to express.
Choosing between the Passé Composé and the Imparfait:

a) In its simplest form, the difference is best thought of as follows:

The Imparfait is a line representing an amount of time during which something was going on; the Passé Composé is a point along the line where something else happened:

_____I was reading.
                                ^
Quand il est entré, je lisais. (When he came in, I was reading).

b) Sometimes neither of the actions is 'finished', so both verbs are Imparfait:
_____My parents did some shopping.
_____I waited in the car.

Pendant que mes parents faisaient des courses, j'attendais dans la voiture.
(While my parents did some shopping, I waited in the car).

c) Sometimes, apparently the same verb is in both tenses:
D'habitude elle achetait Le Figaro, mais ce jour-là elle a acheté Le Monde.
(She usually bought Le Figaro, but that day she bought Le Monde).

Exercice 92 - a

Decide which Past Tense would be used in each of these sentences, if they were expressed in French:
1. I listened to that tape yesterday.
2. When they arrived I was watching television.
3. He rode horses on Sundays until his 50th birthday.
4. They slept while Marthe worked.

Exercice 92 - b

Traduisez l'exercice 92 - a en français. (To ride = Faire du cheval)

Finally, take any opportunity of practising, since practice and experience are easily the best ways of getting these Past Tenses thoroughly understood.

93. Faire faire - Getting things done!

J'ai fait réparer ma Mobylette. (I've had my moped repaired).

Simply use the required tense of Faire, followed by an Infinitive:

On fait venir le médecin? Shall we call the doctor?(i.e. get the doctor to come)

Exercice 93 - a

Exprimez en français:
1. She's had the t.v. mended.
2. I'd like to have the grass cut. (to mow the lawn = tondre la pelouse)

You may have any (sensible!) number of Infinitives after an initial verb:

You're going /to have to/have/ [the mower] /repaired.
Tu vas devoir faire réparer la tondeuse.

Exercice 93 - b

Make up 3 sentences, using faire + Infinitive: One past, one present, one future.

Finally, take a look at SE faire + Infinitive. It means,'to get things done to oneself'.

Je vais me faire couper les cheveux - I'm going to get my hair cut.
Il ne faut pas se faire prendre! - You don't want to get caught!

94. Different meanings of 'Self': Reflexive and «-même»

Il s'est lavé. (He washed himself)
Il a lavé la voiture lui-même. (He washed the car himself).

The Verb in the first sentence is Reflexive, but the '-self' in the second is emphatic - it stresses the fact that it was he (and no-one else) who washed the car.

Emphatic -Self in French is:

Strong Pronoun	+	-même
moi-même		nous-mêmes
toi-même		vous-mêmes
lui-même		eux-mêmes
elle-même		elles-mêmes
soi-même		

Exercice 94 - a

Give the English for each emphatic pronoun (e.g. moi-même = myself)

Exercice 94 - b

Which of these sentences have a Reflexive Verb, and which need -même?
1. She hid herself.
2. She hid the broken glass herself.
3. John looked at himself in the mirror.
4. John did not believe her, so he looked himself.

Exercice 94 - c

Traduisez Exercice 94 - b en français.

To hide (oneself)	(se) cacher
The (pieces of) broken glass	les éclats de verre
The mirror	la glace

95. Le Conditionnel   (The Conditional Tense)

Mon frère payerait les billets, mais il n'a plus d'argent.
(My brother would pay for the tickets, but he hasn't any more money).

Used much as in English, it is formed from:

Future Stem	+	Imparfait Endings:
payer	+	*ait*

If you need to check on these, see 16, 91 and 92. You cannot use these tenses confidently until the basic LEARNING has been done, unfortunately.

You are already used to one Conditionnel:

Je voudrais - I would like

It is from Vouloir (Irregular Future Stem + normal Imparfait endings).

N.B: There are no exceptions to the above, so, once you know the Future and Imparfait, this should be quite easy.

Uses: Similar to English, and used a lot after Imparfait clauses:

Si on rentrait maintenant, on verrait la nouvelle voiture.
If we went home now, we would see the new car.

(*Voir*'s Irregular Future stem is: *verr-*).

Exercice 95 - a

Copiez, en écrivant les verbes entre parenthèses au Conditionnel:
1. Marie-Claire (aller) au cinéma si elle pouvait.
2. Tu (avoir) de la chance, si tu gagnais.
3. S'ils venaient nous voir, on les (inviter) à manger.
4. Si on avait des raquettes on (jouer) au tennis.
5. Si Paul avait le téléphone, il te (parler) plus souvent.

Exercice 95 - b

Traduisez vos réponses à l'exercise 95-a en anglais.

96. Ouvrir to open   and similar Verbs

ouvre	ouvrons
ouvres	ouvrez
ouvre	ouvrent

Participe Passé: ouvert
Racine du Futur: ouvrir-

Verbs following the same pattern:

Couvrir	to cover
Découvrir	to discover
Souffrir	to suffer
Offrir	to offer / give

97. Several / a few / some / a little

These tend to get confused even in English! Try to remember the following:

Several (more than a few but not many)	plusieur
A few (used with COUNTABLE nouns)	quelques
A little (used with UNCOUNTABLE nouns , and adjectives)	un peu (de)

Some

a) (e.g. some butter):   du / de la / de l' / des
b) (= a few): quelques; Quelques minutes plus tard (Some minutes later.

Exercice 97

Ecrivez en français:

1. Some milk.   2. A few weeks later.   3. Several months.
4. A little difficult.   5. A little wine.

98. So / Such a ...

Elle est si haute, une telle tour est difficile à imaginer.
(It's so tall, such a tower is difficult to imagine).

'So + Adjective / Adverb' in French is:
    Either   si   (+ adjectif / adverbe)
    Or   tellement (+ adjectif / adverbe).

'Such a + Noun' is:

(Singular)   une telle (f) (+ nom)
              un tel (m) (+ nom)
(Plural)   de telles (f)
              de tels (m)

'Such a' can also mean 'similar', which is:

        pareil (m)   pareille (f)
        (plurals: add -s)

Je n'ai jamais vu une chose pareille. I've never seen such a thing.

'Such' can sometimes really mean 'so much', when it is: tant:

Il y avait tant de bruit - There was such a noise.

99. Rire   to laugh   Sourire   to smile

ris	rions
ris	riez
rit	rient

Participe Passé: ri
Racine du Futur: rir-
Sourire, to smile, follows the same pattern.

100. Craindre   to fear   and similar Verbs.

crains	craignons
crains	craignez
craint	craignent

Participe Passé: craint
Racine du Futur: craindr-

Verbs following the same pattern as Craindre:

Peindre	to paint
Joindre	to join (something together)
Rejoindre	to join (e.g. one's friends); to get back to (a road)
Eteindre	to turn off (e.g. anything electric); to extinguish
Plaindre	to pity
Se plaindre	to complain.

101. Y and En: Uses, Meanings and Position summarised.

Y = there (in or to that place) / to it.

Elle va au cinéma > Elle y va   (She goes there / She goes to it).

ATTENTION! Because Y means TO it, it can replace all phrases beginning with «à». Look at the following example, where you have «à» in French, but you don't have 'to' in English, so you must watch out.

Marcel pensait au film.	>	Marcel y pensait.
(Marcel thought of the film.	>	Marcel thought of it).

Consider also one or two well-known phrases with « y »:

Il y a - There is/ there are;   Allez-y!   Go on!/ Get a move on!

Vas-y!   Go on!/ Get a move on!

En   = of it / of them /(some/ any) - from it / from them

J'ai trois kilos de pommes   >   J'en ai trois kilos.

(I've got 3 kilos of them).

Tu veux encore des carottes?   >   Tu en veux encore?

(Do you want some more of them?)

ATTENTION! In English - as you can see in the last example - you ould happily leave out 'of them'. In French, you MUST have « en » to make complete sense. **Secondly**, note that En can replace any phrase beginning with « de » (and therefore du, de la, de l', des).

The POSITION of Y and En in a sentence is the same as for an Object Pronoun (See 11, where Y and En are included in the tables).

Exercice 101 - a

Copiez ces phrases, en remplaçant les mots soulignés par Y et EN:
1. Nous allons <u>au théâtre</u> ce soir.
2. Nous allons au théâtre <u>à Amiens.</u>
3. Tu as <u>de l'argent?</u>
4. Réfléchissons <u>aux problèmes.</u>
5. J'ai oublié mes clés <u>au Syndicat d'Initiative.</u>

Exercice 101 - b

Write five short sentences of your own in French, each containing a group of words beginning either with « à », or with « de », or any of their derivatives (au, du, etc.). Then rewrite them using Y and EN instead.

102. Dont   and   Duquel etc. (Of which; Whose)

Je suis désolé, les dépliants dont vous parlez ne sont plus disponibles.
(I'm sorry: the leaflets you're talking about aren't available anymore).

Le rocher du haut duquel on voyait l'hôtel...
(The rock from the top of which you could see the hotel...)

You may well come across these expressions in things you read or hear, so you need to undertand them.

Dont   means   of which, of whom and whose
...and is always spelt the same way.

duquel de laquelle desquels   desquelles

all mean the same things as « dont », but have to be used   instead of « dont » if there is a prepositional phrase before:

Wrong: la voiture dans l'arrière dont (the car in the back of which..)
Right: la voiture dans l'arrière de laquelle (the car in the back of which..)

Exercice 102

Traduisez en anglais:
1. La dame dont il parlait était la maman de Jean-Claude.
2. La maison des fenêtres de laquelle il se penchait (was leaning)
     était celle (see 63) de ses voisins.
3. Je crois que c'est la moto dont Papa a pris la photo hier.

103. Le mien le tien le sien etc.

Celui-là? C'est le mien. (That one? It's mine).

These are the Pronouns meaning: mine, yours, his, hers, one's etc.

His / Her /

	Mine	Yours	One's	Ours	Yours	Theirs
M. S.	le mien	le tien	le sien	le nôtre	le vôtre	le leur
F. S.	la mienne	la tienne	la sienne	la nôtre	la vôtre	la leur
M.Pl.	les miens	les tiens	les siens	les nôtres	les vôtres	les leurs
F. Pl.	les miennes	les tiennes	les siennes	les nôtres	les vôtres	les leurs

Exercice 103 - a

Copiez et complétez avec le Pronom qu'il faut:
1. Sa chemise est bleue, mais (mine) est verte.
2. Leur appartement est grand, (ours) est un peu plus petit.
3. Notre facteur est sympa, et (yours)?*
4. Je n'aime pas tellement ma bicyclette, je préfère (yours)!*
5. (His), ça va, mais nos disques sont super! (un disque)

* In No. 3, the person you are talking to is 'vous'; in No. 4, you are talking to someone you'd call 'tu'. What difference will that make to the words you use for 'yours'?

Exercice 103 - b

Inventez cinq phrases pour donner des exemples de ces Pronoms.

104. Vivre   to live

vis	vivons
vis	vivez
vit	vivent

Participe Passé   :   vécu
Racine du Futur   :   vivr-

Vivre has not quite the same meaning as the English verb 'to live'. Consider these examples:

Il vit toujours à Paris.	He's still living in Paris.
But: Il est toujours vivant.	He's still living (i.e. alive).

105. Suivre   to follow   Also: Poursuivre, to pursue

suis	suivons
suis	suivez
suit	suivent

Participe Passé	:	suivi
Racine du Futur	:	suivr-

If there is any confusion with '*je suis*', meaning 'I am', there are other ways to express oneself:

Je suis le voleur (!)   >   Je suis en train de suivre le voleur.

Poursuivre follows the same pattern as *Suivre*.

106. Agreement of Past Participles with Preceding Direct Objects (PDO)

Les vacances que j'ai passées en Vendée étaient formidables.
(The holidays which I spent in the Vendée were fantastic).

Les vacances (f. pl.) preceeds the Passé Composé Verb refering to it, so the Past Participle (passé) has to agree with it and -*es* (f. pl.) must be added: ...*passées*...

NOTICE how this is a little clearer when the same sentences are first shown with nouns and then with Pronouns (which preceed the Verb) in the Passé Composé:

J'ai regardé la télévision.   >   Je l'ai regardée.
On a cherché ses clés.   >   On les a cherchées.

In these examples, the Fem. Sing. and Fem. Pl. endings can clearly be seen.

Agreement endings are, as usual: Fem. Sing: -e   Fem. Pl: -es
                                         Masc.Pl: -s

Occasionally, the endings double the length of the Past Participle!:

Les pâtisseries que j'ai vues...   The pastries which I saw...

Exercice 106

Rewrite, adding agreement endings if necessary:
1. Les soeurs de Paul, que j'ai rencontré hier, adorent le tennis.
2. Maman, que tu as vu à la maison, vient nous chercher plus tard.
3. Les cartes que nous regardions étaient vieilles.
4. Avez-vous écouté les disques que je vous ai prêté?
5. Ils ont fermé les campings à minuit.

107. Pronouns: Position when there are more than one

Je donne la carte à maman   >   Je la lui donne.
(I give the card to mum   >   I give it to her).

Just a reminder to check Section 11. The first Triangle shape shows the order in which you should put Pronouns if there are more than one.

The example above shows how *la* and *lui* (in this case, 'it' and 'to her') are placed in the right order before the Verb « donne ».

Referring to 11, try the following exercise:

Exercice 107

Remplacez les mots soulignés par des Pronoms:
1. Elodie lance le ballon à son cousin.
2. Tu passes la confiture à Philippe, s'il te plaît.
3. J'ai rencontré tes copines à l'hôtel.
4. Vous voulez voir le film à Nantes?
5. Il a envoyé les lettres à son oncle.

108. Pronouns in Negative Sentences

J'ai cherché mes dossiers, mais je ne les trouve pas.
(I've looked for my files, but I can't find them).

Order: ...NE + Pronoun + Verb Expression including PAS

   ...ne   les   trouve   pas

Stick to this formula even when the Verb expression looks more complicated (for example, in the Passé Composé):

Tu ne les lui as pas donnés? - You didn't give them to him?

Exercice 108 - a

Placez correctement les Pronoms:
1.   On n'enverra pas.   (leur les)
2.   Vous ne devriez (should) pas montrer.   (lui la)
3.   Ne donne pas!   (me le)
4.   Elle n'a pas chanté.   (la nous)
5.   Ne dis pas!   (le leur)

Exercice 108 - b

Traduisez vos réponses à 108 - a en anglais.

109. Expressions of Measurement

Elle a 47m de long sur 18m de large./Elle est longue de 47m et large de 18 m.
(It's 47m long by 18m wide).

a) AVOIR + Measurement + de + long / large / haut (no agreement) ('by' = « sur »)
b) ETRE + Adj (agreeing) + de + Measurement.

« Profond » (deep) is a little different:

La piscine est profonde de 2m.   The pool's 2m deep.
or La piscine a 2m de profondeur.   (Profondeur = depth).

c) Descriptions: A 60 metre garden: Un jardin DE 60 mètres (de long).

d) Personal Height / Weight: Mesurer / Peser

He's 1m 80 tall	Il mesure 1 mètre 80.
He weighs 75 kg	Il pèse 75 kilos.

Exercice 109

Give your own height in French, then describe a house you know well by giving its height, width and length (approximately, of course!) in proper expressions as shown above. Use metres.

110. The Passé Simple (Past Historic Tense) – A Brief Introduction

Elle se frotta les yeux, s'essuya les mains et se mit à débarasser la table. (She rubbed her eyes, wiped her hands and began to clear the table).

You do not need to be able to write in this tense for GCSE (or even most Scholarship exams at 13 + at present). However, it is a tense used in stories of all kinds, and even in newspaper reports. You therefore should have a rough idea of what it looks like, and so avoid being put off if you come across it. As you can see from the examples, the Passé Simple is a one-word tense, and most Verbs can easily be recognised in it.

se frotta	is from frotter, to rub
s'essuya	is from essuyer, to wipe
se mit	is from se mettre à, to begin to, and is a little less easy because « mettre » has a slightly irregular Passé Simple form.

Here are the Passé Simple forms of commonly-used Verbs which you might not be able to guess so easily:

être	je fus	(I was)
avoir	j'eus	(I had)
faire	je fis	(I did, I made)
vivre	je vécus	(I lived)
naître	je naquis	(I was born)

Exercice 110

Write in English what you think these expressions mean:
1. Il naquit le 14 juillet, 1938.
2. Nous mangeâmes en vitesse.
3. Elles furent là, à la porte.
4. Il me fit entrer dans le magasin.
5. Charles se précipita chez le docteur.

111. Subjunctive: A Brief Explanation.

> Mais que voulez-vous que je fasse, alors?
> (But what do you want me to do, then?).

Much more often used in French than in English, in all written and spoken situations, the Subjunctive (like the Passé Simple) needs at least to be recognised and understood, if possible, especially beyond GCSE.

Note the different structure:

	What do you want me to do?
becomes:	What do you want <u>that I do?</u> ...in French.

Subjunctive phrases are always introduced by the word « Que », so the Verb forms are usually listed that way in reference books.

Here are some Subjunctives you would hear almost every day in conversation, at the very least:

être	qu'il soit	Je veux qu'il soit gentil - I want him to be good.
faire	que je fasse	Tu veux que je fasse la cuisine?
		- Do you want me to do the cooking?
aller	qu'on aille	Il faut qu'on aille tout de suite- We'd better go right now.
avoir	que tu aies	Je ne veux pas que tu aies du mal à nous trouver - I don't want you to have trouble finding us.
savoir	que je sache	Il préfère que je sache pas quel âge il a - He prefers that I don't know his age.

Others are much easier to understand, because most of them sound (and look) exactly like the Verbs they come from. If you know your Present Tenses, you should have no trouble at all, as they mostly sound like the « ils » part (except Nous and Vous forms, which are like the Imparfait):

> Voulez-vous que je prenne le bleu ou le rouge?
> (prenne is clearly from Prendre, and sounds like « prennent »)

> ...so you probably know the question means:
> Do you want me to take the blue one or the red one?

Exercice 111

Traduisez en anglais:
1. Ma grand-mère voulait que je réfléchisse.
2. Il faut qu'elle parte avant minuit.
3. Il ne faut pas que nous arrivions trop tôt.
4. Didier demande qu'on vienne fêter son anniversiare.
5. Elle ne veut pas qu'on sache qu'elle l'aime.

As you can see, Subjunctives appear when there is uncertainty, hope or fear in the idea which follows.

However, one 'hoping' Verb - espérer - ('to hope' itself) is *not* followed by the Subjunctive.

> J'espère que tu viendras (Futur) à Noël.

112. Avant de... + Infinitif

Frappez avant d'entrer, s.v.p. (Knock before entering, please).
Avant de + Infinitive = before ...ing.

Exercice 112 - a

Exprimez en français:
1. Before going home.
2. Before leaving.
3. Before eating
4. Before cleaning the sail-board.
5. Before having supper.

Avant de + Infinitive may also be used to avoid other Verb tenses:

Avant de faire la vaisselle, il a allumé la radio.
(Before he did the dishes, he turned on the radio).

Exercice 112 - b

Inventez cinq autres exemples et traduisez-les en français.

113. Le Plus-que-Parfait (The Pluperfect Tense)

Ils étaient arrivés, mais ils n'avaient pas encore déchargé le coffre.
(They had arrived, but they hadn't yet unloaded the boot).

Used much as in English, this compound tense is formed the same way as the Passé Composé (45 and 73), using the Imparfait of Avoir/Etre instead of the Present, but all the same Past Participles:

J'avais trouvé	- I had found	(Trouver goes with Avoir)
J'étais resté	- I had stayed	(Rester goes with Etre).

Exercice 113

Ecrivez en français:
1. We had finished the ice-creams.
2. Marie-Christine had not seen the film.
3. Pierre's father had written to his aunt.
4. You hadn't noticed the road-sign? (le panneau routier)
5. She'd asked Sophie's brother. (Remember: demander à)

114. Sans + Infinitif

Elle était partie sans fermer les fenêtres.
(She had left without shutting the windows).

Sans (without) is followed by an Infinitive to mean: Without '...ing.'

Exercice 114

Exprimez en français:
1. Without finding.   2. Without seeing.   3. Without reading.
4. Without knowing.   5. Without discovering.

When this construction has after it the sense of '(not) any', e.g. "Without putting on any gloves," the word « de » is added, as the sense is almost like « pas de...»:

Sans mettre de gants.

115. Aucun / Aucune

Combien de buts as-tu marqués? - Aucun.
(How many goals did you score?- None).
Il n'y avait aucune maison occupée d'un bout de la rue à l'autre.
(There wasn't a single house occupied from one end of the street to the other).
Aucun is like « pas » in meaning, but also expresses: none; not any.
It may be used to begin a sentence, but still needs « ne » before any Verb it goes with:

Aucun élève n'était présent ce jour-là.
(No pupil / Not a single pupil... was present that day).

116. De Plus en Plus / De Moins en Moins

Il est de plus en plus difficile de trouver un bon restaurant ici.
(It's more and more difficult to find a decent restaurant here).

These expressions can intensify Adjectives or Adverbs:

De moins en moins difficile   (Adj.)
De plus en plus vite   (Adv.)

Note the Irregulars:

Better and better: de mieux en mieux
From bad to worse: de mal en pis

Exercice 116

Traduisez en français:
1. She sings better and better.
2. They drive faster and faster.

If « Ça va » is used for things being 'O.K.', how would you say:

3. Things are going from bad to worse!

117. Ce Qui... and Ce Que

Ce qui m'embête, c'est qu'il réussit ses examens sans bosser.
(What annoys me, is that he passes his exams without swotting).
Oui, c'est ce que je lui ai dit.
(Yes, that's what I told him).

Ce Qui is a Subject phrase (like « qui »)
Ce Que is an Oject phrase (like « que »)   -see Qui/Que, 62.

The real meaning of both phrases is: that which, but we prefer 'what' in English these days. You should now know the following ways to say 'What':

Que   Que fais-tu? / Qu' est-ce que tu fais? (Question)
Ce qui (as explained above)

Ce que

Quoi   Il faisait quoi, alors? (Question, where 'what' is put at the end for emphasis)

Quoi?   (Expression of surprise: What?)

Other meanings arise from idioms where 'what' in English is not 'what' in French:

Comment t'appelles-tu?   What is your name? (Real meaning: How?)
Quel jour est-on?   What day is it?   (Real meaning: Which?)

Exercice 117

Exprimez en français:
1. What you told me is true.
2. What did I tell you?
3. You told me what Richard had said to Simone.
4. What is their house called?
5. « Migwen ». What a funny name!   (a funny ... = drôle de...)

118. Adjectif + de / à + Infinitif

Elle était prête à partir.   (She was ready to leave).
Vous êtes certain de le trouver chez lui.   (You're sure to find him in).

Adjectives which are linked to following verbs (easy to find etc.) have either « à » or « de » after them.

Try to learn each one as you come across it. Here are a few examples:

difficile à trouver   difficult to find
facile à faire   easy to make
bon à manger   good to eat
prêt à partir   ready to leave

Below are two with « de », these generally being followed by an Object or Complement:

C'était difficile de faire des progrès.   It was hard to make progress.
Je suis content de venir ici.   I'm happy to come here.

Exercice 118

Make a list of ten Adjectives in French. See if you can add a suitable Infinitive to them (which would be found in normal use), and put « à » or « de » with each one, keeping as close as you can to the guidelines above. Give the English for your examples.

119. Inversion and when to apply it.

- M'attendez-vous depuis longtemps? nous a-t-il demandé.
(Have you been waiting for me for a long time?" he asked us).

After quoted speech, and in simple questions, the subject and Verb are Inverted.

If the Verb is Compound (made up of more than one word, like the Passé Composé), it is the Avoir or Etre part which is inverted with the person:

Il dit	>	dit-il
Il a dit	>	a-t-il dit

There are alternatives to Inversion in Questions:

M'attendez-vous?
    or: Est-ce que vous m'attendez?
    or: Vous m'attendez? (Tone of voice only).

Exercice 119 - a

Copy, completing with a correctly inverted Verb form:

Exemple: Bonjour!(Elle a crié) > Bonjour! a-t-elle crié.

1. Bonsoir, (Il a dit)
2. Toujours en vacances? (Il a demandé)
3. (Vous avez terminé) votre repas?
4. (Ils étaient rentrés) avant votre retour?
5. (Il va) en ville.

NOTE: what happens to Inversion if a name is mentioned:

Ça va? (Paul a demandé) > Ça va? a demandé Paul.
Papa ve en ville   > Papa va-t-il en ville?

Exercice 119 - b

Refaites l'Exercice 119 - a, en écrivant Sébastien (au lieu d' « il ») et Tes frères (au lieu d' « ils »).

120. Directional Verbs with Present Participles showing Movement

Il est entré en courant.   (He ran in).
Literally, He went/came in, running.
In French, the sense of the phrase 'He ran in' is conveyed by « Entrer » fo 'going in', and by « EN » and the Present Participle of « Courir » for 'running'

Exercice 120 - a

Traduisez en anglais:
1. Mélanie est sortie en courant.
2. Il a monté la rue en courant.
3. James s'est sauvé en courant.   (se sauver = to get away)

Exercice 120 - b

Traduisez en français:
1. She ran downstairs.
2. Colette and Maria ran up to the policeman.

Fin de la Première Partie

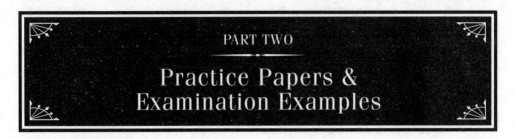

PART TWO

Practice Papers &
Examination Examples

Each **practice paper** on the following pages is complete in itself. It may be used as a **homework task**, set as a test or prepared in advance, as a **teaching resource**, for use and discussion during lessons,or for **revision** of exam techniques.

The papers may be split up and the various **writing** and **reading** exercises tackled separately.

Throughout, the emphasis is on the student's **understanding** of the form and function of the elements of the French language he or she will have to cope with in the first four years of French study towards GCSE, particularly with any sort of Independent Senior School Scholarship exam in view. Added to this is the goal of getting students to **think,** and to **apply** and **use** the language, so they may **express** themselves successfully and accurately, with confidence.

The papers are arranged so that the earliest ones should be tackled by the youngest students. The earliest papers contain some exercises designed primarily to prompt a little thought, whereas the later ones reflect current exam styles more closely.

The subject matter in the papers is, I hope, comprehensive and a practical compromise between popular GCSE courses and the current format of Common Entrance and scholarship exams.

Papers are marked to show roughly which yeargroups ought to be able to tackle them. This will vary from school to school, but because in Independent prep-schools, children tend to start French at a different age from the children in maintained sector, I have simply indicated in which year of French study the pupil should be.

Paper 1: *2nd Year of French*

Juste pour mettre le pied dans l'eau!

GENERAL EXERCISES

1. Copy, filling in the missing months:

    janvier, ..., mars, ..., mai, juin, ...,.............,
    septembre, ..., novembre, ...

2. Copy this list, putting the right English opposite each date:

    le jour de l'an
    Pâques
    la fête nationale
    Noêl

3. Copy these expressions, putting the right endings on the verbs:

    a. Elle port...... une belle robe noire.
    b. Tu trouv...... ton cahier?
    c. Nous cherch........des fraises.
    d. On regard........ la télé ce soir?
    e. Non, je préfèr....... écouter mes disques.

4. Write sentences about yourself which answer these questions:

    a. Quel âge as-tu?
    b. C'est quand ton anniversaire

5. Give the French for:

    a. a black dress
    b. a white skirt
    c. a (pair of) green trousers
    d. red socks
    e   a blue tie

6. You arrive in a French town. Which sign would direct you to the tourist information office?

    a. Gare SNCF
    b. Syndicat d'Initiative

c. La Poste
d. La Piscine Municipale

7. Below is a conversation between person A and person B. Read it then answer the questions which follow it.

A   Pardon monsieur, pour aller à la poste, s'il vous plaît?
B   Il y a un bureau de poste près d'ici, madame, rue des Saules. Vous allez tout droit sur deux cent mètres, puis vous prenez la deuxième à droite.
A   Merci monsieur, est-ce qu'il y a un tabac là?
B   Il y a un tabac Place du Marché.
A   C'est loin?
B   Non madame, ce n'est pas loin. Vous voulez acheter des timbres?
A   Non, je veux acheter des cartes postales.

1. Is person A a man or a woman?
2. Which place does person A want to find first?
3. What must person A do to get there?
4. What does B think A wants to buy?
5. Is the newsagent's shop a long way?

8. Write the French for these expressions:

some butter some bread some cheese some salad   some coffee
some wine   some milk   some tea   some chocolate   some lemonade

9. Write **two** different English versions of these expressions :

de l'eau minérale du sucre   des petits pois
de la viande   des frites

10. You have to know how to give your opinion of French cooking! Reorder these expressions so that the last expression you write shows you like the food most.:

c'est délicieux   c'est bon   c'est très bon

11. Now match the following expressions to the correct English:
j'aime ça   j'aime beaucoup ça je n'aime pas beaucoup ça
j'adore ça   je n'aime pas ça

I like it / I don't like it / I love it / I don't like it much /
I like it a lot.

12. Write four sentences in which you say at what times you have meals.
Start each sentence with: On prend (we have), add the name of the meal, then
give the time.

    Exemple: On prend le (.........) à (.........).

13. Write out the irregular verbs Aller, Etre, and Faire in full, giving the
English for their infinitives, but not for each part.

    Exemple: ALLER to go
                je vais
                tu (etc.)

14 Write these expressions with the English opposite in the correct place:

je prends	as vegetables there are
je mange	I'm drinking
je bois	for dessert we have
comme légumes il y a	I'm eating
comme dessert nous avons	I'm having

15. You go into a Supermarché, hoping to buy some cold meats for your
picnic. Which sign do you look for?

    boucherie   charcuterie boulangerie bricolage

16. Write the correct part of Avoir for each gap. No need to copy the whole
sentence.
    a.   Suzanne, est-ce que tu .... ma liste?
    b.   Non, maman, je n'.......... pas ta liste.
    c.   Est-ce que Christophe et Jean-Claude .... la liste?
    d.   Non, ils n' .... pas la liste.
    e.   Ah, c'est le bébé qui .... la liste!

17. Write the correct part of the right verb which would go in these brackets.
Use the verbs vendre, attendre, descendre, or répondre:

    a.   Suzanne (gets off) de l'autobus à la gare.
    b.   Je (am waiting for) mon ami Christophe.
    c.   Pourquoi est-ce que tu ne (answer) pas à ma lettre?
    d.   Mon père (sells) des jeux électroniques.

PAPER 2: *2nd Year of French*

On se met en route!

APPROACHING EXAM-TYPE QUESTIONS

1. *Read Jean-Luc's description of a typical day, then answer the questions below it in English:*

D'habitude je quitte la maison à sept heures et demie. Je vais au collège avec ma mère en voiture, et j'arrive au collège à huit heures moins dix.

Mes cours commencent à huit heures, et on mange à midi vingt. Je rentre à la maison à conq heures vingt-cinq,et je mange le dîner avec ma soeur et mes parents. Quand j'ai des devoirs à faire, je ne regarde pas la télé.

Je vais au lit à huit heures et demie.

1. At what time does he leave home?
2. How does he get to school?
3. What happens at ten to eight?
4. At what time do lessons begin?
5. Who has the evening meal with him?
6. When does he <u>not</u> watch t.v.?
7. What does he do at 8. 30 p.m.?

2. *Read the passage then answer the questions that follow in English.*

Moi, au petit déjeuner, je prends des toasts avec de la confiture d'oranges, ou, le dimanche, des croissants. Je bois du chocolat chaud, sauf en été: en été je ne prends pas de chocolat, je préfère boire du jus de fruits. J'ai un ami anglais qui prend des oeufs au bacon et des céréales, et qui boit du thé, mais sa soeur Joanna mange "à la française". Ma soeur est idiote: elle ne mange pas au petit déjeuner, et elle dort en classe - zzzzzzzz!

1. What does the writer of this passage have for breakfast?
2. When does he have croissants?
3. When does he <u>not</u> have hot chocolate?
4. What sort of breakfast does his friend have?
5. What does the writer think is the reason why his sister falls asleep in class?

3.　　*Copy, rewriting the jumbled-up words as fruits or vegetables:*

　　　1.　　J'aime les (safires).
　　　2.　　Les (spetti sopi), j'adore ça!
　　　3.　　Mon légume favori, c'est les (ostricha trevs)
　　　4.　　Je voudrais une (riepo) s'il vous plaît.
　　　5.　　Je n'aime pas beaucoup les (neasnab).

4.　　*Write a shopping list in French for a picnic.*

　　You will need: about half-a-pound of cheese, some bread, two bottles of mineral water, a kilo of peaches, some butter, eight slices of ham, two packets of crisps and some lemonade.

5.　　*Devinettes (guessing game). Read the descriptions of these items of clothing then decide what they are. For each one, write a sentence beginning:*

　　　　　　　　　C'est un(e).....................

　　　1.　　Les femmes et les filles mettent ça, mais pas les garçons! C'est chic.
　　　2.　　On met ça quand on va au lit.
　　　3.　　C'est un petit vêtement que l'on met avec une chemise.
　　　4.　　On met ça quand il pleut.
　　　5.　　On achète ça en paires, mais ce ne sont pas des chaussettes.

6.　　*What should you say? Write the* <u>correct</u> *sentence in full, leaving out the wrong word.*

　　　1.　　What shall I wear? - Qu'est-ce que je (fais / mets) ?
　　　2.　　His mother is here. - (Son / Sa) mère est ici.
　　　3.　　What would you like? - Qu'est-ce que vous (demandez / désirez) ?
　　　4.　　They have calculators. - Elles (avez / ont) une calculatrice.
　　　5.　　He sells fish - Il (vend / vends) le poisson.

Paper 3: *2nd Year of French*

READING COMPREHENSION

1. *Read this letter then answer in English the questions that follow.*

Saint-Laurent, le 31 septembre

Cher Jim

     Merci de ta lettre du quinze août. Ça fait déjà trois semaines que je fais de l'anglais au collège. Je l'aime bien mais je ne suis pas encore très fort. Le prof d'anglais est sympa, mais j'ai du mal à bien prononcer les mots.

     Heureusement c'est samedi demain, je vais aller chez mon oncle et ma tante qui habitent au bord de la mer. On se promène sur les plages tous les jours, et on ramasse des moules qu'on prépare le soir pour le dîner. C'est chouette.

     A bientôt,   Paul.

1. How long before this letter had Jim written?
2. How long has Paul been learning English?
3. What does he think of the teacher?
4. How easy does he find English pronunciation?
5. Where is the writer going on Saturday?
6. What does he do there?

2. *You find a mini-golf course near your camp-site and decide to try to read the rules on the back of the score-card. Answer the questions in English.*

PARCOURS DE GOLF-MINIATURE

–   Ouvert tous les jours sauf: le lundi et jours fériés, de Pâques à la Toussaint, de 11h à 20h.
–   Tarif 1995: Adultes 32 F   Enfants de moins de 12 ans 16 F

RÈGLEMENT

–   Partez du départ et suivez le parcours dans l'ordre indiqué des trous 1 à 18.

-   Jouez sur la piste sans y mettre le pied.
-   Si l'un des joueurs ne réussit pas après six coups de club, il marque 7 sur la fiche et la partie continue.
-   Le/la gagnant(e) est celui ou celle avec le plus petit total après 18 trous.
-   En cas de balle perdue, ou coincée, renseignez-vous au bureau d'accueil.

1. What does the first instruction tell you to do?
2. When is the mini-golf course open?
3. How much would a party of 2 adults, one child of 7 and a 13 year-old have to pay?
4. What must you <u>not</u> do?
5. What does a player do if he/she fails to sink the ball in 6 shots?
6. When should you go to the office to seek help?

WRITING EXERCISES

1. *From question 1 of the Reading Comprehension*, find the French for:

    a. I've been doing English for three weeks already.
    b. I'm going to go.
    c. I'm not very good yet.
    d. I find it difficult to...

    Now work out the French for:

    e. I've been reading for two hours already.
    f. She's not going to go.
    g. We're quite good (at something).
    h. He finds it hard to speak.

2. *Write a short message saying:*

    1. that Paul's been at your house for two days;
    2. that he's going to stay for two weeks;
    3. that he's quite good at English...
    4. ...but he finds it difficult to understand the t.v.

Paper 4: *2nd/3rd Year of French*

READING COMPREHENSION

1.   *This is an extract from a letter you have received from France, in which your correspondant Paul talks about decorating the house. Read it, then answer the questions which follow.*

...Mon père est en train de refaire la peinture des murs de ma chambre et de celle de ma soeur. Elle, elle veut qu'il achète du papier peint avec des chevaux dessus, bien sûr. Moi, je n'aime pas ça, je préfère les voitures de course. De toute façon, papa dit que cela ne va pas durer; qu'au bout d'une année elle ne va plus être passionnée de chevaux, et qu'elle va exiger quelque chose de différent.
    Papa dit qu'il est content qu'elle ne s'intéresse pas encore à la mode, ni aux garçons!

(exiger - to demand)

1. What is Paul's father doing at the moment?
2. What does his sister want instead of paint?
3. What would Paul prefer?
4. Why does their father think it's not worth getting what his sister wants?
5. Why is their father happy (according to the last paragraph)?

2.   *While you are staying with your correspondent in France, a leaflet is slipped into the letter box. The Word 'T-Shirt' catches your eye, so you decide to see what it is all about. Read the following, then answer in English the questions below:*

JOELLE MOD'

Vêtements de Confection pour toute la Famille

–   SPÉCIAL VACANCES:
        10% de réduction sur toute la gamme de vêtements de sport d'hommes et sur toute tenue de ski d'enfants
–   NOUVEAU!
        Achetez deux T-Shirts "P'tit Mec" et vous en recevrez le troisième gratuit! (Offre valable jusqu'à la fin du mois de février).

1. Who would benefit from the 10% price cut in sportswear?
2. What sort of children's clothing is reduced?
3. What special offer is in force?
4. When does the offer finish?
5. Who do you think the T-shirts are for?
6. Give one reason for your answer to No. 5.

WRITING EXERCISES

1. *From question 1 of the Reading Comprehension, find the French for:*

   a. ...and my sister's one (i.e. the one belonging to my sister).
   b. She wants him to buy...
   c. After a year is up,...
   d. ...she isn't yet interested in...

   Now work out the French for:

   e. ...and my brother's.
   f. I want him to eat.
   g. At the end of a week.
   h. ...they're not interested in...

2. *Write a short message saying:*

   1. that you like your bedroom but you prefer your brother's;
   2. that you don't want your parents to buy wallpaper with racing cars on;
   3. that, at the end of a month, you'll no longer be interested in racing cars.

Paper 5: *2nd/3rd Year of French*

READING COMPREHENSION

1. *You are at a restaurant in France, and your parents ask you to explain the munus to them. Read them then answer the questions below.*

MENU A 58 F	MENU ENFANTS A 32 F

Crudités ou Potage fermière
ou Assiette anglaise

Carottes rapées

~

Entrecôte au poivre garnie
ou
Plateau de fruits de mer

Poisson pané
ou
Steack hâché
frites

~

Fromages au choix

Glace ou tarte aux pommes

~

Glace ou tarte aux pommes
ou
Fruit saison

VINS

Pichet 50cl Rouge
Blanc
} 45 F

Café
Boissons non-compris

Pichet 25cl   25 F
Côtes du Rhône   97 F
1/2 bt   65 F

Using French or English phrases as necessary, suggest menus for the following people:

1. Your 75-year-old grandmother who can eat neither meat nor cheese.
2. Your little brother of 7, who hates fish.
3. Your father, who cannot eat raw vegetables, doesn't like fish, and wants something fresh for dessert.
4. Suggest a wine. Not only is your mother driving (so they don't want very much), but also: they don't like white wine and don't want anything too 'fancy'.

2. *The following brief history is found inside the front cover of the menu.
Answer in English the questions which follow it.*

Ce restaurant se trouve 22, Place de la République, depuis 1934, date de
l'achat du bâtiment original par les grands-parents du propriétaire actuel.
Détruit par les bombardements aériens des Alliés lors du débarquement
de 1944, c'est M. Castillon, architecte de la ville, qui se charge de sa ré-
construction après la guerre. M.Castillon est un ancien camarade de classe
du propriétaire, M. Chiron.

1. Where is the restaurant?
2. Since when has there been a restaurant on this site?
3. Who were its first owners?
4. How did it come to be destroyed?
5. How does the present owner know M. Castillon?

WRITING EXERCISES

1. *From the Reading Comprehension passages, find the French for:*

   a. of your choice
   b. not included (in the price)
   c. is situated in the Place de la République
   d. ...who sees to
   e. an old friend

   Now work our the French for these expressions:

   f. (an) ice-cream of your choice
   g. bread not included
   h. the garage is situated in the Rue des Saules
   i. It's Pauline who sees to the wine
   j. the old owner.

2. *Write a short message (no longer than a postcard) in which you:*

   1. say that you'd like to go to the "Louis Philippe";
   2. say that it's Monsieur Laidet who sees to the cooking*;(*la cuisine*)
   3. say that it's situated in the village;
   4. that your uncle is an old friend of the present owner.

Paper 6: *2nd/3rd Year of French*

READING COMPREHENSION

1. *Read this extract from a letter, then answer the questions below in English.*

Cher Luc,   le 6 juillet

Demain, c'est la fête du lac ici à Apremont. On organise des jeux et des courses aquatiques, c'est super. Tout le monde qui habite au village ou dans les environs y participe ou vient regarder. Il y a de la danse folklorique mais c'est surtout les plus âgés qui le font: pour les jeunes il y a un bal-disco champêtre et on mange en plein air.

Le soir il y a un grand feu d'artifice sur le lac. On regarde le spectacle reflété dans l'eau. Cela commence à la tombée de la nuit, vers 23 heures, car on ne voit pas bien s'il fait encore jour. C'est beau, j'espère que tu vas venir.

1. On what date is the Fête du Lac?
2. What is organised apart from games?
3. Is it limited to to villagers of Apremont?
4. Who generally participates in the folk-dancing?
5. What happens late at night?
6. What makes this particularly beautiful?

2. *Study the following cinema adverts then answer in English the questions which follow them.*

REX 22 h 30
Les Histoires de la Crypte (2) (A): Le Financier.
    Film allemand en v.o. avec sous-titres. Le directeur d'une banque
    tue la femme de son meilleur ami...
                        Interdit aux moins de 18 ans

DRAGON 16 h 30   18 h 30
Marciana '43 (It)
    Film italien; dialogue français. Une quinzaine de plongeurs,membres
    de l'équipage d'un sous-marin britannique, se préparent pour placer des
    bombes magnétiques sur la coque d'un bateau allemand dans le port
    italien en pleine nuit...

XYZ - 3 Salles Climatisées

1   Dodo et le Petit Nuage (Fr)   16 h 30   17 h 30
     Dessin animé pour les enfants

2   Le Cadran Enchanté (USA)   18 h 30   20 h 30
     Fantaisie américaine en version originale

    1.   Your penfriend's 19 year-old sister has a German friend staying next week. Which film would you suggest for them to see?

    2.   Your penfriend doesn't like war films or cartoons, and is 12. Which film would you expect him to choose, and why?

    3.   Which film would be acceptable to a British tourist who spoke neither French nor German?

    4.   What sort of person would you take to see 'Dodo et le Petit Nuage?'

WRITING EXERCISES

1. *From the Reading Comprehension passages, find the French for:*

    a.   games are organised
    b.   In the evening
    c.   it's still light
    d.   in the open air
    e.   for young people

Now work out the French for these expressions:
    f.   lessons are prepared
    g.   In the morning
    h.   it's still dark
    i.   in the open sea (Attention! sea is feminine)
    j.   for older people.

2. *Write a short message (no longer than a postcard), in which you:*

    1.   say that next week it's the Mountain Festival;
    2.   say that ski races are organised*;
    3.   say that there's a disco in the evening for everyone;
    4.   say that it's too cold to eat in the open air on the mountain.

In this case, 'ski' should be: 'de neige'.

Paper 7: *2nd/3rd Year of French*

READING COMPREHENSION

1.   *You are reading "Animaux sans -abri" in a magazine. Read the following advertisements the answer IN ENGLISH the questions which follow.*

Cochon d'Inde gentil et doux répondant au nom
de Yoko, qui a deux ans. Tél: 23.45.67.89
après 16 heures.

Chatons sages et mignons
vaccinés. Téléphonez au
31.32.34.25. de 11h à 15 h.

Petit chien gentil, marron noir et
blanc. Tél: à partir de 19 heures
au: 24.32.25.56

  1. What animal is Yoko?
  2. If you were phoning 31.32.34.25, what sort of animal would you be interested in?
  3. What colour is the dog?
  4. When can you phone about Yoko?
  5. If you could only get to a phone after 4 p.m., which animals could you
       not hope to adopt?

2.   *You have received this letter. Read it and answer IN ENGLISH the questions which follow.*

Cher (...),   Toulon, le 12 novembre

Merci de ta dernière lettre. Ça me fait très plaisir de recevoir une lettre
d'Angleterre. Comment vas-tu? Moi, ça va. Quelle est la date de ton
anniversaire? Moi, c'est le dix-huit août. Quel jour tombe ton anniversaire?
Moi, cette année, c'est un mercredi. Comment passes-tu ta semaine en
Angleterre? Je vais te raconter ma semaine classique:

Le lundi, ah, je déteste les lundi. Je dois aller à l'ecole. Je travaille toute
la semaine au college, sauf le mercredi. Le mercredi, je ne travaille pas,
je joue au foot avec mes copains. Le samedi, c'est chouette, je sors avec
maman et papa. On va en ville ou à la piscine. Le dimanche, je dors
beaucoup. D'habitude je suis très fatigué après une semaine d'école.

Cette année j'ai passé un quatorze juillet génial. Le quatorze juillet, tu sais, c'est la Fête Nationale en France, et pour les vacances de la Toussaint, on est allé à l'île Maurice. Il fait très très chaud là-bas, mais au moins on parle français. C'est bizarre, là-bas il est minuit quand il est neuf heures du soir ici.

Bien, je dois finir. La poste ferme dans 5 minutes (il est 6h 55) et je dois acheter des timbres.

A bientôt

Ton ami

Benoit

1. What is Benoit pleased about in the first 2 lines?
2. What date is Benoit's birthday?
3. Which two questions does he ask about your birthday?
4. Why does Benoit dislike Mondays?
5. Which day of the week does he not have to go to school on?
6. What does he like about Saturdays?
7. What does he often do on Saturdays?
8. What does Benoit say about Sundays?
9. What date is the French national holiday on?
10. At which time of the year did Benoit go to Mauritius?
11. According to Benoit, what is a major difference between France and Mauritius?
12. What time-difference is there (according to this letter) between France and Mauritius?
13. What similarity is there between France and Mauritius?
14. Why must Benoit go to the post office?
15. What time does the post office close?

3.   *These rules for being safe as a pedestrian have become muddled up in the computer. Write down the **letter** of each one you think is in the WRONG column. For example, if you think 'z' is in the wrong column, write: z.*

LE BON PIETON   LE MAUVAIS PIETON

a. Je joue sur le trottoir.   f. J'attends le petit bonhomme vert
b. Je regarde derrière moi.   g. Je traverse en courant.
c. Je marche dans la rue.   h. Je traverse au passage piéton.
d. Je joue dans la rue.   i. Je discute sur un passage piéton.
e. Je regarde à droite et à gauche. j. Je cours dans la rue.

These Writing Exercises for **Paper 7** are not like those you have seen up to now. To give you a taste of exam-style work, they are not, unlike Papers 1 to 6, related to the Reading Comprehension questions. You will find that the same is true for the last papers in the 12 year-old section, as well.

WRITING EXERCISES

1.   Shorter Task.   *You are organising a party.   Write a list of ten things that you will be getting for people to eat and drink.Your list must be in FRENCH.*

---

2.   Longer Task.   *You are writing to a French friend, telling him about the coming weekend, when he is coming to your house.In your letter you must:*

1.   Thank him for his letter.
2.   Say what animals you have and ask him if he has any.
3.   Suggest going to a restaurant that you know, when he comes.
4.   Say what you are going to have if you go there.
5.   Tell him where it is and how to get there.

---

3.   Exercise.   *Copy the paragraph out and fill in the gaps with the best possible word from the choices given below.*

Quand j'invite des .... à la maison, nous ne
.............pas la télévision, nous ....des...............
et quelquefois nous................ Le .... de mon
anniversaire, j'.................une boum à la maison
avec .... parents. Je fais un gâteau, mais je ne
suis pas ...., alors je ne mets .... de
chocolat dessus!

*organise   dansons   pas   mes   copains   regardons   cassettes
écoutons   gourmand   jour.*

Paper 8: *3rd Year of French*

READING COMPREHENSION

1. *Read this extract, then answer in English the questions which follow it.*

La semaine dernière, on est allé faire une randonnée en montagne. Nous avons passé le plus clair de notre temps à parcourir la forêt: c'est une région où toutes les collines sont couvertes de bois. On y cultive des sapins pour vendre à Noël, mais de moins en moins, car on commence à penser aux forêts qui disparaissent... Après trois heures de marche, nous nous sommes arrêtés pour manger au pied d'un grand rocher gris d'où on a pu voir une cascade d'eau. Moi, j'ai eu deux sandwichs au pâté et ma soeur a avalé un paquet entier de petits gâteaux! Nous avons bu de l'eau, mais pas beaucoup, parce qu'il a fallu la garder pour plus tard. Maman a dit qu'on ne sait pas si l'eau de la montagne est bonne.

1. When did they go walking?
2. What was the landscape like?
3. What are the pines in this forest grown for?
4. Why are they beginning to do less of this sort of thing (see No. 3)?
5. Where did they have lunch?
6. What could be seen from there?
7. How do we know they had a good appetite?

2. *Read the following information leaflet about visits to a château, then answer in English the questions below.*

Le Château est ouvert de 10 h à 12 h 30, et de 15 h à 19 h tous les jours, sauf le mardi, du 1er avril au 30 octobre.

Visitès du Chàteau:
Tarif unique : 25 F   Enfants de moins de 12 ans accompagnés : gratuit

La visite n'est pas conseillée aux enfants de moins de huit ans.

Visite guidée possible le samedi et le dimanche.

Pour toutes visites de groupes scolaires ou de personnes handicapées, prière de nous prévenir au moins une semaine à l'avance si possible.
La visite se termine dans la boutique de souvenirs, où vous trouverez des cartes postales, des livres, des affiches représentant les tableaux ainsi que des cartes historiques du Château et de la Vieille Ville.

1. The château re-opens after lunch at what time?
2. On which days of the week is it open?
3. How much would you have to pay to get in if you were 11, and you were with an adult who had already paid?
4. What is said about children under 8?
5. What is available at the weekend?
6. How much notice do they need for school parties?
7. Who else do they need advance warning for?
8. Give 3 things that may be bought in the shop.

WRITING EXERCISES

1. *From the Reading Comprehension passages, find the French for:*

   a. we went for a walk
   b. they grow fir-trees there
   c. covered in woods
   d. it's not known if the water is good
   e. please warn us

   Now work out the French for these expressions:

   f. we went for a car-ride
   g. they grow vegetables there
   h. covered in snow
   i. it's not understood
   j. please ask us

2. *Write a letter thanking your penfriend for his / her last letter, and giving an account of your recent holiday. You must include the following:*

   1. an account of your journey;
   2. a description of a walk you went on;
   3. something about a picnic you had;
   4. what you thought of a château you went round;
   5. what souvenirs you bought (for any two members of yourfamily).

Paper 9: *3rd Year of French*

READING COMPREHENSION

1. *You have found the description of a new building near where you are staying. Read it and answer the questions which follow in English..*

    Le bâtiment est composé de deux sections reliées par un couloir de quinze mètres de long. Chaque section possède un sous-sol, un rez-de-chaussée, et deux étages. Du côté sud (face à l'autoroute) il y a les salles de classe de langues vivantes, et, de l'autre bout du couloir (côté prés), vous avez les laboratoires. La fonction des sous-sol n'a pas été déterminée, mais on parle de bibliothèques, et de salles de jeux intérieurs en cas de pluie.
    Il y a quatre escaliers et un ascenseur, aussi bien pour l'équipement que pour les quelques étudiants qui se servent de fauteuils roulants.

    1. What joins the two parts of the building?
    2. How many floors are there, apart from the basement?
    3. What can be seen from the south-facing wing?
    4. What faces the meadows on the other side?
    5. Which part of the building hasn't had its use decided yet?
    6. What are the suggestions for its use?
    7. What will be the main uses of the lift?

2. *Read the following poster and answer the questions beneath in English.*

LA SECURITE ROUTIERE EN VILLE

Suite à plusieurs accidents et la mort d'un jeune touriste dans le village l'année dernière, la Comité des Jeunes de Saint-André vous propose ces conseils. Profitez au maximum de votre séjour en les observant:

1. Marchez face à la direction de la circulation des véhicules.
2. Avant de traverser la rue, regardez à gauche d'abord, puis à droite plusieurs fois.
3. Ne traversez une rue qu'aux passages piétons.
4. Ne sortez pas le soir sans prendre de lampe de poche: les rues ne sont pas éclairées après 22 h.
5. Au lieu de tournez à gauche à bicyclette, descendez au bord de la route et traversez-là à pied.

1. Who has drawn up these guidelines?
2. Why were they drawn up?
3. When there is no pavement, which side of the road should you walk on?
4. Which way should you look when crossing a road?
5. What is said about pedestrian crossings?
6. What should you take with you at night when going out?
7. What is the reason given for this?
8. What advice is given to cyclists?

WRITING EXERCISES

1. *From the Reading Comprehension passages, find the French for:*

   a. linked by a 15m corridor
   b. on the south side
   c. hasn't been decided
   d. in case of rainy weather

   Now work out the French for these expressions:

   e. linked (m) by a staircase
   f. on the north side
   g. hasn't yet been found
   h. in case of fog

2. *Using the expressions in the passage to help you, write a description of a building bearing in mind the following points:*

   1. It has 3 parts joined by one staircase;
   2. The west part has mathematics classrooms in it;
   3. The ground floor will have the offices (les bureaux)

3. *Write a short set of guidelines in French for young visiting French people to walk or cycle safely on British roads in a town. Include:*

   1. advice on crossing roads;
   2. something about not going out alone at night;
   3. what to do at a pedestrian crossing;
   4. something about (cyclists) turning right on British roads.

Paper 10: *3rd Year of French*

READING COMPREHNSION

1. *Below is most of a letter rom an English boy to his French pen-friend Read it then answer in ENGLISH the questions below:*

    (...) Je me suis levé très tôt ce matin parce que j'ai un autre correspondant––Philippe–qui va arriver ici dans quelques heures! Il va passer quelques jours ici, et je vais l'accompagner quand il rentre en France. C'est pour ça que je t'écris maintenant.
    Je suis tellement fatigué car je me suis couché très tard hier soir; j'ai regardé une cassette vidéo dans ma chambre (maman n'en sait rien, bien entendu!) avant de m'endormir. Ce matin il faut tout ranger dans la chambre de ma soeur pour Philippe qui va y coucher. Sandra va partir chez son amie à Winchester.
    Et toi, est-ce que tu vas en vacances de neige à Méribel, comme d'habitude, ou est-ce que tu vas faire autre chose? Quand vas-tu venir à Portsmouth? Philippe habite au Touquet. Je suis content d'y aller, il y a des tas de magasins de jeux électroniques et de maquettes.

    > En vitesse,
    > amitiés,   Ben.

    1. Why is Ben up early?
    2. Why did Ben go to bed late?
    3. What must he do this morning?
    4. Where will Ben's sister be for the next few days?
    5. What question does Ben ask about Méribel?
    6. What does he ask about Portsmouth?
    7. Why does Ben look forward to going to Philippe's home town?
    8. What is Philippe's town called?

2. *On holiday in France, you go to the local swimming pool to check on the times and prices. Read the following then answer in English the questions that follow.*

PISCINE ET GYMNASE RIBAULT

> Ouvert de 8h à 22h sans interruption. Fermé le jeudi.
> Prix de l'entrée: 18 ans et plus: 30F Moins de 18 ans: 15 F
> Le ticket d'entrée permet la participation à toute

activité pendant toute une journée.

Suppléments cours particuliers:

    Natation: 25 F/h Groupe de 10 minimum*

    Gymnastique: 25 F/h Groupe de 10 minimum*

    Tennis: 50 F/h (1 pers) 30 F/h (2 pers) 20 F/h

                  (3 pers) (Prix par personne)

* S'adresser au bureau d'accueil situé au rez-de-chaussée

1. How long is the sports hall closed for lunch?
2. How many days a week is it open?
3. What does the entry ticket entitle you to?
4. How much would 2 of you, under 18, have to pay for two hours tennis coaching, including the entrance fee?
5. What do you do first if you want to arrange swimming lessons?

WRITING EXERCISES

1. *From the Reading Comprehension passages, find the French for:*

   a. in a few hours
   b. that's why I'm writing to you
   c. Mum knows nothing about it
   d. before going to sleep
   e. there are masses of shops.

   Now work out the French for these expressions:

   f. in a few days
   g. that's why he's angry
   h. I know nothing of it
   i. before leaving (going away)
   j. there are masses of games.

2. *Write a letter in which you tell your penfriend about what you'll be doing in the next few weeks. You must:*

   1. say what time of day it is (as you write);
   2. say that when you've finished the letter you'll be tidying the garage with your dad / mum;
   3. say what you did last night;
   4. say where you are going in the next few days;
   5. ask your correspondant 2 questions.

Paper 11: *3rd Year of French*

READING COMPREHENSION

1. *You are looking at some notices in the Town Hall, all about people who have gone missing. Read the descriptions then answer the questions which follow IN ENGLISH.*

Recherche FARDEAU Marie-Annick
22 ans; mesure 1m 65; pèse 48 kilos;
de taille moyenne; cheveux courts et
bruns; yeux verts. Tél: 21.34.54.54.

DUVAL Robert 24 ans; sportif;
aux cheveux roux et bouclés;
assez grand (1m 80); pèse 84 kg;
portant pullover vert et jean bleu
Téléphonez au: 21.34.55.56

Je m'appelle Michèle, je ne suis pas
retournée à la maison après une belle
journée à la piscine. Mes parents sont
très inquiets. J'ai les cheveux longs et
blonds, j'ai les yeux gris et je porte
des lunettes. J'ai 14 ans. Trouvez-moi
vite s.v.p! Tél: 21.34.77.87

1).   How much does Marie-Annick weigh?
2).   Give two details about her hair.
3).   Whose age is given as 24?
4).   What was Robert wearing when he was last seen?
5).   How is Robert's height described ?
6).   What was Michèle last known to be doing?
7).   What colour are her eyes?
8).   What colour is Robert's hair?
9).   What distinguishing feature does Michèle have that may help to identify her?

2. *You receive the following letter from a friend in France. Read it, then
    answer IN ENGLISH the questions which follow it.*

Cher (...)   le 14 mai

    Merci de ta lettre que j'ai reçue hier. Ça fait déjà trois mois que je suis
à la maison après ma visite en Angleterre chez toi, et c'est la première lettre
que tu m'écris!
    Nous n'avons pas de chance, mes parents, ma soeur et moi. Moi, je
passe tout mon temps chez le docteur. J'ai mal au bras et au genou, ma mère
a mal au dos, c'est parce qu'elle travaille beaucoup dans le jardin. Papa, il
est au lit en ce moment, il a mal à la tête. C'est possible qu'il aime trop le vin
rouge de mon oncle Jules! Ma soeur, elle est enrhumée, elle fait tout pour
s'en sortir: elle boit du lait chaud avec du miel dedans, elle porte de gros
pulls même qu'il fait chaud, mais elle a toujours le rhume.
    Notre maison est comme un hôpital! Le chien, Toby, il va très bien!
    Il faut que je te quitte maintenant, je dois aller à la pharmacie pour
les médicaments de la famille. J'espère que tu vas bien!

    Écris-moi vite.
    A bientôt,   Sylvain

1).   On what date did Sylvain receive your last letter?
2).   What is wrong with Sylvain?
3).   Why has his mother got backache?
4).   What is the matter with Sylvain's father at the moment?
5).   What does Sylvain give as a possible reason for this?
6).   What has his sister done to try to get rid of her cold?
7).   What does Sylvain say about Toby, the dog?
8).   Why does Sylvain say he has to finish the letter now?

3. *Read the following then answer the questions IN ENGLISH;*

Marc est plus grand que Sophie mais moins grand que Gérard.

Les cacahuètes Bisou sont aussi chères que les chips Merveille, mais plus
chères que les Apérinoix.

Le Pays de Galles est plus petit que la France.

1).   Who is the taller out of Marc and Gérard?
2).   Which is the cheapest snack?
3).   Is the final sentence true or false?

4.   *Read the following extract from Pauline's diary then answer in ENGLISH the questions below.*

Lundi	Je fais les courses pour maman.
Mardi	On va au complexe sportif - Formidable!
Mercredi	Nous allons chez mon oncle et ma tante.
Jeudi	Je fais du judo et nous allons à la piscine.
Vendredi	Je fais mes devoirs, après avoir dîné.
Samedi	Je reste au lit toute la journée!

1).   What does Pauline do on Monday?
2).   On which day does she go to the swimming pool?
3).   Which activity does she seem to enjoy most?
4).   When is she going to her aunt and uncle's house?
5).   When does her homework get done?

Here is another, rather 'different' set of writing tasks, just to bring in the element of the unknown you get in an exam.

WRITING TESTS

1. Shorter Task.   *Your French friend's puppy has run away. While he looks for it, you write a notice to pin up. Your notice must include the following:*
   (N.B. Lost Puppy = Chiot Perdu)

   1.   Say what the puppy's name is.
   2.   Say whether he is big or small.
   3.   Say what colour he is.
   4.   Give the colour of his eyes.
   5.   Give your friend's phone number (in the French style)

2. Longer Task.   *You are writing a letter to a French friend. In it, you decide to tell him about how you spend a normal day and compare it to a normal day of your brother, who is lazier than you! In your letter you must:*

   1.   Say what you do, and at what times, before you go to school in the morning.
   2.   Say what time your brother gets up.
   3.   Give three things you do during a normal day.
   4.   Say what you do when you get home.
   5.   Ask your friend what time he does (any) two things.

Make sure you have begun and finished your letter correctly.

Paper 12: *3rd/4th Year of French*

READING COMPREHENSION

1. *Your parents run a hotel in England, and they receive a letter from a French family. They ask you the questions below. Read the letter, then answer the questions in English.*

Monsieur, Madame,

   Nous serons de passage par votre village au mois de juillet, et voudrions nous y arrêter une nuit (le 10) en arrivant en Angleterre. Pouvons-nous donc réserver: une chambre à un grand lit avec douche, et une chambre à deux petits lits pour les enfants.
   Notre projet est de passer également par St. Lawrence en redescendant, la nuit du 21 juillet, avant de prendre le car-ferry le lendemain à huit heures. Il faut demander la possibilité de nous servir le petit déjeuner très tôt, mettons à 6h, pour qu'on arrive à temps au port.
   Dans l'attente d'une réponse de votre part, nous vous prions de croire, Monsieur, Madame, à nos sentiments les meilleurs.
   Arthur et Joséphine DAGUERRE

1. How long will they sepend at your hotel when they arrive?
2. What sort of room do the parents want?
3. How many children are there?
4. What suggests that they plan to go north for their holidays?
5. What date will they take the ferry to go back home?
6. What special request do they need to make?

2. *You are looking at your air ticket. You have lost the English notes going with it, and only have the French ones left. Read through them and answer the questions below in English:*

- Prière d'arriver au moins une heure et demie avant le départ de votre vol.
- Veuillez vous présenter au bureau de contrôle et déposer vos bagages au moment de votre arrivée.
- Gardez soigneusement vos bagages à main et surveillez toujours vos valises avant de les déposer.
- Toute valise laissée sans surveillance sera enlevée et peut être détruite.
- En cas de perte, renseignez-vous au bureau d'information.
- Le bar-restaurant fermera une heure après le départ du dernier vol de la journée, et définitivement à 23 h.

1. Your flight is at 13.00. When should you arrive by?
2. What two things should you do first on arriving at the airport?
3. What is said about hand-luggage?
4. What <u>might</u> happen to unattended luggage?
5. What <u>will</u> happen to unattended luggage?
6. What should you do if you lose something?
7. What is said about the restaurant?

WRITING EXERCISES

1. *From the Reading Comprehension passages, find the French for:*

    a. we'll be passing through
    b. a double bed
    c. on our way back down
    d. before taking the ferry
    e. at least an hour and a half

   Now put these expressions into French:

    f. she'll be going through Paris
    g. a single bed
    h. on our way up
    i. before going home
    j. at least two and a half weeks

2. *While you are alone in the house of your French friends, there is a telephone call, of which you write down the details. A certain Monsieur Pleyel rang to say:*

    1. that he's taking the 7 p.m. flight;*
    2. he asks if you (the people you are staying with) can meet him at the information desk;
    3. that he has three cases and some hand luggage;
    4. that he hopes to be there on time.

    *('the flight of 7 p.m.' Don't forget French people use the 24-hour clock, so you don't say 7 p.m.)

PAPER 13: *3rd/4th Year of French*

READING COMPREHENSION

1. *Read the following letter, then answer IN ENGLISH the questions which follow. It is from a French-speaking friend of yours.*

Cher Steve,   Montréal, le 24 octobre

    J'ai reçu ta lettre il y a une semaine, j'espère que la mienne arrive vite chez toi. Donc, comment est la vie en Angleterre? Chez moi il commence à faire froid. Quel temps fait-il en Angleterre? J'ai reçu des tas de lettres de mes amis qui habitent dans d'autres pays, comme toi. Ils ont tous des vies différentes à la vie canadienne. Par exemple, il y a Maya qui habite au Sénégal. Là-bas, les enfants ne vont à l'école que le matin, et l'après-midi on reste à la maison. Il paraît que, le jeudi, on range tout dans la maison et tout le monde donne un coup de main.

    Moi aussi, je dois aider à la maison. Je m'occupe de la pelouse. Je tonds la pelouse avec la tondeuse et je vais au garage chercher de l'essence pour le moteur. En plus, j'aide mes parents à laver la voiture. Comme ça je 'gagne' mon argent de poche. Et toi, tu dois travailler à la maison? Reçois-tu de l'argent de poche? Moi, j'en reçois deux dollars par semaine.

    Bon, il faut que je te quitte. N'oublie pas de m' écrire et de me raconter ta vie en Angleterre.

    A bientôt,
      Etienne

1. How long ago did Etienne receive your letter?
2. What does he ask about first?
3. What is the weather like where he lives?
4. When do children in Sénégal go to school?
5. What happens on Thursdays, according to this letter, in Sénégal?
6. What does Etienne do to help at home?
7. What sort of mower do they have?
8. What does Etienne receive in return?
9. What does Etienne finish his letter by asking Steve to do?

2. *You are reading a French friend's magazine. You come to the 'problem page' where teenagers write about their troubles and worries. Read the letters and answer the questions IN ENGLISH.*

Cher Pablo,
J'ai peur, surtout quand j'ai
un examen. J'ai une boule
dans la gorge. Aidez-moi!

Georges

Cher Pablo,
Je n'aime pas le noir, et la lumière
reste allumée dans ma chambre
toute la nuit. Je dors mal et je suis
toujours fatigué.

Pascal.

Cher Pablo,
J'ai du mal à retrouver mes
affaires. Je ne suis pas
organisé et j'en souffre parce
que l'on se moque de moi.
Que dois-je faire?

Marcel

1. When does Georges get most worried?
2. What effect does this have upon him?
3. What is Marcel's worry?
4. Why does he suffer so much from it?
5. What fear does Pascal have?
6. How does he try to cope with this fear?
7. What result has this had?

3. *Reading on, you come across this article. Answer the questions that follow in
   ENGLISH.*

Un Noël Pas Comme les Autres

Cette année nous avons fêté Noël comme d'habitude, mais pour nous c'était un
peu triste, et pas du tout comme un Noël normale. Mon frère n'était pas là,
il faisait un stage pour lequel il devait partir en Angleterre pendant deux mois,
donc on était juste maman et moi à la maison. Après avoir passé le matin chez
une amie, je suis rentrée pour préparer le repas de midi. On a mangé des
carottes rapées, un poulet rôti comme plat principal, une bûche de Noël, et
une salade des fruits. On a bu un bon Bordeaux, et on a regardé un match
de rugby à la télévision. Mais ce n'était pas un 'vrai' Noël. On n'a pas mangé
de pâté de foie gras, ce que mon frère aime le plus. Le soir à 20 heures
à la télé, on a fait passer un reportage sur la Noël chez les autres. Il y a Fa'ïd
qui habite à Alger. Il a dit qu'on ne fête pas Noël dans son pays, parce
que c'est un pays musulman. Ils ont d'autres fêtes, par exemple le mois de
Ramadan. On n'a pas le droit de manger pendant la journée.
En Australie, on prend le repas de Noël dans le jardin, il fait trop chaud pour
manger à l'intérieur! On prépare un barbecue sur la plage!
(Un stage = a course)

1. Why did the girl who wrote the article find last Christmas a bit sad?
2. What was her brother doing?
3. How did she spend Christmas morning?
4. What did they have as a starter?
5. What did they <u>not</u> have, which they would normally have had?
6. What was the t.v. programme about?
7. Why does Fa'ïd not celebrate Christmas?
8. What are you not allowed to do during Ramadan?
9. What (according to this article) is strange about Christmas in Australia?

WRITING TESTS

1. *Write a short message to your French friend, who is not up yet, to say you have gone out. Say:*

   1. that you have had breakfast;
   2. that you are going into the village...
   3. ...to buy some postcards;
   4. that you are coming back at midday;
   5. that you have tidied your room.

2. *Write a letter to the family of your French friend, to thank them for the week you spent with them at Easter time. Your letter must be properly begun and ended, and include the following:*

   1. say what you are doing at school (i.e. exams);
   2. ask them if your friend (give him a name) also has exams;
   3. say what you had to eat on Easter day in England;
   4. say that your sister is upset at the moment, because...
   5. ...someone at school took her calculator.

3. *Write a short account in French for the school magazine of your French friend, who has asked you about the differences between your life and his. In your article you must:*

   1. give your school's name and say where it is;
   2. say something about the sport(s) you do in the summer term;
   3. say what you most like doing and why;
   4. say what you least like doing and why;
   5. explain how you spend your pocket money at the school shop.

Paper 14: *3rd/4th Year of French*

READING COMPREHENSION

1. *The following is part of a leaflet for tourists describing a French town. Read it, then answer the questions below in English.*

Saint Philippe-les-Bains se trouve dans le sud-est de la France au pied des Alpes. On peut y aller directement par la Route Nationale 365 et cette petite ville charmante n'est pas trop loin des aéroports de Nice (à deux heures de route) et de Genève (à une heure 45). C'est une station de vacances idéale pour tous les goûts: ici on peut faire du ski et pratiquer tous les sports de neige en hiver, mais les vacanciers d'été trouveront également beaucoup de choses à faire: des randonnées à pied et à cheval dans la forêt, des promenades en bateau sur le lac où on peut aussi faire du ski nautique, de la voile et de la planche à voile.

Pour les parents et tous ceux qui préfèrent le calme, pourquoi ne pas faire un pique-nique au bord du lac ou balader dans la vieille ville? Le quartier le plus historique de la ville, qui se compose de ses murs anciens et du Château, date du onzième siècle. Il y a assez de distractions pour les jeunes: la piscine; un cinéma à trois salles climatisées, un bowling et le parc d'attractions à 1 km sur la route d'Aix. Et le soir, n'oubliez pas les restaurants (il y en a 17: on peut choisir entre la cuisine française et européenne, algérienne et vietnamienne), et les discothèques. Visitez les petits bars et cafés pour l'après-ski ou l'apéritif!

1. In which part of France is Saint-Philippe situated?
2. Which is the nearest airport?
3. Why is it a holiday resort "ideal for all tastes"?
4. When does the oldest part of the town date from?
5. What feature does the cinema have?
6. What is decribed as being just outside the town on the Aix road?

2. *Your parents are thinking about a family visit to Paris , and they ask you to explain the following advert they have found in a French magazune. Answer in English the questions below:*

Excursion Spécial Weekend

P A R I S

Passez deux nuits inoubliables à l'hôtel Oxford (***) sur les bords de la Seine

*   *   *

Billet aller-retour 990 F (Demi-tarif pour les moins de 14 ans et les étudiants).

- ☐ Voyage aller-retour 2ème Classe
- ☐ 2 nuits + petit déjeuner
- ☐ Chambre de famille 2 / 3 / 4 personnes.

Les chiens ne sont pas admis. Réservations par téléphone au 46.21.21.21 ou par Minitel : 36.15 OXFORTRAIN.

De toutes les gares S.N.C.F. de la Dordogne du 14 juillet au 15 août.

1. When can you take this excursion?
2. How long can you stay in Paris?
3. Where in Paris is the hotel?
4. Who may travel for a reduced fare?
5. What is included in the price?
6. What does it say about dogs?
7. How can you book your tickets?
8. Where in France must you travel from, to qualify for this offer?

WRITING EXERCISES

1. *Write a short, postcard-style message to some French friends you are going to stay with in which you tell them the following things:*

    1. that you are going to arrive on the tenth of July;
    2. that it is raining at the moment ;
    3. that you will be arriving at Beauvais airport...
    4. ...at half-past three in the afternoon;
    5. and that you are going to be wearing (give 2 items).

2. *Write an article (about 120 words max.), in which you describe a town, real or imaginary, for a school languages club in France. Write in such a way that young people could get some idea of whether they would want to go there. Your article must include the following:*

    1. a description of where the town is;
    2. how you can get there;
    3. what you can do there in summer;
    4. something about the restaurants;
    5. something about a football match between your school and some French visitors.

French: *Towards GCSE*

Paper 15: *4th Year of French*

READING COMPREHENSION

1. *You have just arrived by car in a fishing port in France. Your mother, who is driving, asks you where she should park. The following notices give the information. Read them, then answer the questions below in English:*

   a) **P** 500 m Port de Plaisance > b) **P** Réservé aux plaisanciers de Saint-Gilles
   c) **P** Gratuit > 200 m après 2ème Feu à Gauche
   d) **P** du Centre: Stationnement Payant:
                 Prenez un Ticket à
                 l'horodateur.
                 [8h à 20h sauf le dimanche et jours fériés]
   e) **P** Rue du Maréchal Foch: Zone Bleue: Disque Obligatoire
   f) **P** Place de Vitry.   g) **P** Place du Marché
       Stationnement Payant   Parking toléré tous les jours
       de 8h à 12h 15 et   sauf le 2e et le 4e jeudi du mois
       de 15h à 19h

   1. How far away is the car park for the Marina?
   2. Why can't just anyone park there?
   3. How would you get to the free car park?
   4. Which car-park is free at lunch time?
   5. On which days could you park free in the Parking du Centre?
   6. What do you need, to park in the rue du Maréchal Foch?
   7. Why do you think you can't park on the days shown in No.7?

2. *Zappi is a magazine devoted to teenagers. Readers are encouraged to write in, to seek advice. Read the following letter, then answer the questions which follow, in English:*

Cher Zappi,

    J'ai le cafard parce que j'ai horreur des boums et des boîtes. A l'école j'ai l'impression d'avoir beaucoup d' "amies", mais, les classes finies, elles se moquent de moi, j'en suis sûre, et chaque fois qu'on organise une soirée j'ai le trac même en y pensant. L'autre soir on m'a invitée en boîte, et il y avait pas mal d'assez beaux garçons, mais personne ne m'a parlé et j'ai passé soirée collée aux murs. Ce qui m'embête c'est que j'adore danser, mais il me manque

du courage donc je ne peux plus m'amuser du tout.

Qu'est-ce que tu me conseilles?

Claudine

1. What does Claudine hate?
2. Why does she put the word 'amies' in inverted commas?
3. What makes her nervous, even thinking about it?
4. How did she spend the evening last time she went out?
5. Why did this annoy her particularly?
6. Why does she feel this is happening?
7. What question does she ask at the end of her letter?

WRITING EXERCISES

1. *Write a short message of about 5 lines to your host family, who are not yet up and about, to explain where you have gone, including the following details:*

    1.   you've gone for a walk as you couldn't sleep;
    2.   say you'll be back in an hour;
    3.   say you'll bring the bread with you...
    4.   ...from the bakery on the corner;
    5.   ask if you can go to the beach after breakfast.

2. *Write a letter to a French teenage magazine, to be published in a regular column which deals with young people's problems, and comments on their lives. In your letter (of about 120 words), you must:*

    1.   give two things that you really dislike in life;
    2.   give a recent example of one of them;
    3.   write some details about yourself;
    4.   say what your friends think about your worries;
    5.   ask for some advice.

Finally, list all the new vocab you have come across.

List all the words you're not sure of. Do this yourself; write them down, **research** the meanings and **learn** them.

Paper 16: *4th Year of French*

READING COMPREHENSION

1. *You are waiting in the Tourist Office of the town where you are staying on holiday in France. As you look around, you read these notices. Answer in English the questions below.*

a) Petit train de Noirmoutiers
   Tour de la ville en 45 minutes
   Départ toutes les quinze minutes
   de 11 h à 23 h.
   Tarif: 50 F, enfants 25 F

b) le 24 juillet
   Concours de Pêche
   organisé par la
   Société des Marins Pêcheurs
   de Noirmoutiers
   S'adresser à la Mairie

c) Stella Parc de Saint-Gilles
   Parc d'attractions et de loisirs
   Ouvert du 1er avril au 30 octobre
   de 10h à 20h. Entrée 40 F, tarif
   réduit - groupes scolaires ou de
   plus de 20 pers: 25 F / personne

d) OptiZola
   Votre opticien professionel
   28 Place Emil Zola
   Examen sur rendez-vous de
   15 h à 17 h
   Magasin ouvert de 9h à 12h30
   et de 15h à 19h
   Lunettes - lentilles de contacte
   - Jumelles -
   Téléphone: 00.71.08.94

a) 1. It's 8.30 p.m. and a train is just leaving. When's the next one?
   2. If you set off at 3.00, when will you get back?
b) 3. What sort of competition is it?
   4. Where do you go to get the details for it?
c) 5. In Stella Parc, how much would a family of five pay?
   6. Who gets a reduction?
d) 7. What must you do to get an eye-test?
   8. <u>When</u> can you get an eye-test?
   9. What does the shop sell apart from glasses?

2. *You stay in a rented flat by the sea. The agent gives your parents a leaflet. Read the fiollowing then answer the questions in English:*

   1. La deuxième clé se trouve pendue à l'intérieur du placard à droite en entrant dans la cuisine.
   2. Pour conformer aux conditions exigées par l'assurance, il est obligatoire de garder les volets fermés la nuit et en cas d'absence.

3. Tout ce qu'il faut pour six personnes (couverts, assiettes, tasses, verres) se trouve dans les placards supérieurs et dans les tiroirs de la cuisine. Les casseroles et autres articles de cuisine sont dans les placards inférieurs.
4. Prière de ne toucher ni au régulateur du chauffage central ni au compteur d'eau.
5. En cas de difficulté se renseigner au bureau de l'agence aux heures des repas.

1. What's kept in the kitchen cupboard as you go in?
2. What must you do to comply with insurance regulations?
3. What's kept in the upper cupboards and drawers?
4. Where would you find, for example, a mixing-bowl?
5. What should not be touched?
6. When can you phone, if you need to?

WRITING EXERCISES

1. *Your host family's mum is going shopping. You've forgotten all your washing kit and she asks you to write a list of everything you need, in French, so she can get it for you when she's out. Write a note saying what the list is, and end it by thanking her. You need:*

    a.   soap
    b.   toothpaste
    c.   a toothbrush
    d.   a comb
    e.   something to put them all in.

2. *Write a letter on behalf of your parents, to an agency that rents out holiday homes. In your letter, which must be started and finished in an apprpopriate way, you must:*

    1.   say that last time your parents didn't like the house they rented;
    2.   give two reasons why not;
    3.   give details about the sort of house / flat your family will need;
    4.   say how long you will need it for;
    5.   ask for a brochure with prices etc.

Now make a list of all new vocab you have come across, research it, write it down and learn it.

Paper 17: *4th Year of French*

READING COMPREHENSION

1. *Read the following letter, then answer in English the questions which follow:*

jeudi 4 mars

Cher Sébastien,

   Salut! J'espère que tu vas bien, moi, ça va. Merci de la cassette que tu m'as envoyée. Comme tu sais bien, j'adore le métal, c'est archi-cool, surtout Gagamaschine.

   Dimanche dernier, comme tous les weekends, j'étais en train de distribuer les journaux dans une des rues de notre quartier. Au 14, en laissant tomber un journal dans une boîte à lettres, j'ai senti quelque chose de froid et de mouillé, puis leur chien m'a mordu! J'ai sonné plusieurs fois, pendant que l'animal aboyait férocément. Finalement on est venu m'ouvrir, et, en voyant le sang qui coulait de mes doigts, la dame y a mis un pansement et m'a emmené tout de suite à l'hôpital en voiture. Rien de grave, mais j'ai dû avoir quatre points dans mon indèxe, et une pîqure.
   J'avais complètement oublié les journaux!
N'oublie pas de m'écrire vite!

Pierre-Yves

1. What has Sébastien recently sent Pierre-Yves?
2. What does Pierre-Yves say about Gagamaschine?
3. When did the incident take place?
4. What was Pierre-Yves doing when it happened?
5. What was the first thing Pierre-Yves felt?
6. What did the dog do while Pierre-Yves rang the door-bell?
7. What made the lady do something to help?
8. What treatment did Pierre-Yves need?
9. What does he say finally about the papers?

2. *You see these signs at various places in a hotel restaurant. What does each one mean?*

1. Défense de fumer   2. Espace fumeurs   3. Direction
4. Frappez avant d'entrer   5. Entrez sans frapper

3. *You see these road signs on the car journey. Your parents ask you what they mean. Give their meanings:*

  6.   Travaux sur 2 km
  7.   Déviation poids lourds à 800 m
  8.   Ile Saint-Louis: Suivez file de droite
  9.   Péage à 500 m: préparez votre monnaie.
 10.   Roulez sur deux voies.

WRITING EXERCISES

1. *Having left your penfriend's family the previous day, you have safely arrived with your parents on holiday somewhere else in France. Write a note to your penfriend's family, saying:*

  1.   that you got here at two o'clock in the morning!
  2.   that there was no-one here;
  3.   but that your mum / dad arrived five minutes later...
  4.   ...to pick you up;
  5.   that the weather is marvellous.

2. *Write a letter to a new penfriend in Martinique, who only speaks French. Your letter must imaginatively follow these guidelines:*

  1.   Say something about your age, where you go to school, and which year you are in.
  2.   Ask him / her questions to get the same information as you have just given in question 1.
  3.   Say what sort of music you like, and ask what he / she prefers.
  4.   Say what you hope to do next holidays.
  5.   Ask if he / she would like to come to Europe.

Now list any new vocab, research it, write it down, and learn it.
Don't forget with **verbs**, to check whether they are regular or not, and then to make sure you know all you need to about them:

       their : present tense
            past participle
            whether they go with Avoir or Etre
            future stem
Always check with your teacher if you aren't quite certain.

Paper 18: *4th Year of French*

READING COMPREHENSION

1. *The following interview in a French magazine catches your eye. You decide to see how much of it you can understand. Answer the questions which follow in English:*

Le tour du monde à vélo: Jacques et Line Vrignaud au micro de notre correspondant **Alexandre Giraudoux.**

A.G   Qu'est-ce qui vous a fait décider de faire le tour du monde à vélo?

J.V.   Nous voulions, tout simplement, voir le monde, avant de nous installer dans une vie "normale", acheter une maison, et tout.

A.G.   Cela vous a pris combien de temps?

L.V.   Jacques m'a proposé de faire ça en 1984. Il nous a fallu un an et demi pour faire les préparatifs, donc on est partis de Villeneuve-le-Roi en juin 1985. Au début, notre projet était de faire le tour du monde en trois ans, mais nous ne sommes rentrés en France qu'en août 1994!

A.G.   Quel est le plus grand problème que vous avez rencontré?

J.V.   Le froid. On avait décidé de passer les hivers à traverser les déserts, mais nous ne savions pas à quel point la température baisse, la nuit.

1. What exploit have these people carried out?
2. Why did they decide to do it?
3. How long did it take to prepare?
4. How long did the actual adventure take (without the preparations), to the nearest year?
5. What was their biggest problem?
6. Why was this the case?

2. *You then come across some adverts for penfriends. Read them, then answer the questions which follow.*

MIREILLE, 16 Veux échanger des lettres avec garçons et filles de mon âge. Je suis passionnée de chevaux et de la planche à voile. N'aime pas: la cuisine japonaise, ni ceux / celles qui se plaignent tout le temps / les personnes négatives.

JEAN-LUC,   15 ans Ch. correspondant(e)s de 14 à 16 ans qui aiment la musique classique et les films étrangers. N'aime pas:

le football, la cruauté aux animaux.

PAULINE,   14 ans Cherche une amie qui habite au Canada ou aux Etats-Unis. J'aime: faire des promenades en bateau, jouer du piano. Je n'aime pas: la nostalgie (les gens qui vivent dans le passé), la violence.

1. What age of penfriends is Mireille looking for?
2. What does she really like?
3. What does she say about Japanese food?
4. Is Jean-Luc looking for girls or boys to write to, or doesn't he mind which?
5. What should Jean-Luc's future penfriends be interested in?
6. What does Jean-Luc not like?
7. Where do Pauline's penfriends have to live?
8. What does she like, apart from piano-playing?

WRITING EXERCISES

1. *Compose a penfriend advert about yourself, similar to those above. Make sure you include the following details:*

   1.   your age and where you want your penfriend to be living;
   2.   what you are interested in;
   3.   what you do not like;
   4.   whether you want to write to a boy or a girl or don't mind;
   5.   the age range of your possible penfriends.

2. *Write an article of about 120 words, describing a visit your class made to France. In your article you must:*

   1.   explain the purpose of the visit;
   2.   describe the journey you took to get there;
   3.   describe the place you stayed in;
   4.   say what you enjoyed most about the visit;
   5.   say whether you would want to do the same thing again: if so, why, and if not, why not.

Reminder: Vocab and verbs!

HARDER PAPERS
suitable for preparation for
Scholarship at 13+ to independent senior schools.

It is well-known that different senior schools choose to measure the candidate's skill by different methods. Furthermore, the standard of difficulty in scholarship papers varies astonishingly widely from school to school, certainly in French.

In the following pages, an attempt has been made to give examples of some, though not all, of the different exercises one may be expected to encounter.

A friend of mine once produced a staggering sheet of paper on which the different question styles of all the major independent schools were listed and checked for frequency. One of its main findings was the predominance of comprehension exercises. That was several years ago. As I write, there seems to have been a fairly distinct divergence recently, between those schools whose scholarship French papers are heavily influenced by G.C.S.E., and those whose papers are still very academic, and individual.

Below is a list of the most frequently seen question types in present-day exams.

> Reading Comprehension (English questions and answers)
> Reproduction of a story read out to candidates
> Listening Comprehension (from tape or read out)
> Story writing from brief guide
> Letter / article writing
> Translation into English
> Translation into French

Less frequently seen but still in evidence are:
> Dictation
> Reading Comprehension with French questions and answers
> Story writing from pictures
> Grammar exercises ('Use of French')

Several other styles are used, and no judgment is intended here on which are 'good' questions. It is important to remember that senior school examiners will find out what they want to know about a candidate from *any* question.

The Oral: Oral exams vary as well, but most include a straightforward interview with the candidate. Some might require him or her to prepare a rôle play exercise or 'situation', so that a specific range of language may be tested comparatively.

What follows is a series of test papers which may be used for their exercises or as complete exams. As indiciated at the beginning of the book, oral and listening work are not covered here, except in some example 'situations' and advice on oral exams in general.

Paper 19: S

EXERCISE 1

Copy each of the following expressions, then write next to it the same thing in the tense indicated:

J'ai voulu	(imparfait)
Il voit	(passé composé)
Nous étions	(présent)
Tu prends	(futur)
On sait	(imparfait)
Je m'arrête	(passé composé)
Nous verrons	(présent)
Ils ont reçu	(présent)
Il n'y a pas	(passé composé)
Tu enverras	(plus-que-parfait)

EXERCISE 2

Rewrite the following, filling each gap with a suitable word, to make the sentence make sense:

1. J'adore la robe [   ] tu m'as achetée ce matin.
2. Paul m'a prêté son stylo, mais je ne le [   ] ai pas rendu.
3. Attention! Tu as laissé tomber [   ]parapluie!
4. Allô? [   ] est à l'appareil?   Ah, c'est [   ], chérie.

5. J'ai essayé [   ] trouver [   ] photos de ma soeur, mais
    je [   ] ai complètement perdues.
6. Quel temps [   ] - il? J'espère qu'il va [   ] beau plus tard.

EXERCISE 3

Read the following article, then answer the questions which follow. Be careful to follow the instructions.

Paris: bagarre dans un bureau de change

A la suite de l'intervention d'un policier, hier soir, un "hold-up" dans un bureau de change s'est terminé avec trois morts. Le policier, qui n'était pas en service au moment de l'incident, se trouvait dans la boutique par hasard vers 15h 45, lorsque les trois malfaiteurs sont arrivés sur scène.

Se sentant menacé, et ayant peur (selon lui) pour les employées du bureau et leur patron, le policier a sorti son arme de sa poche et a tiré sur les trois agresseurs . L'un des trois est mort sur le coup, les deux autres sont morts à leur tour quelques heures plus tard, malgré les efforts des médecins et des sapeurs-pompiers.

Le policier a été interrogé pendant une heure, il paraît que ce dernier était très traumatisé par ce qui venait de se passer.

L'enquête aura lieu le plus tôt possible, l'Inspection générale des services s'en chargeant. On prétend que le fait que le policier a tiré six fois risque de changer cet acte d'autodéfense en homicide involontaire.

1. Where did this incident take place?
2. When did it take place?
3. Was the policeman on or off duty?
4. What made him take action?
5. How many people were killed or injured in the incident?
6. What was the effect on the policeman?
7. Give the meanings of the following phrases:

    a.   à la suite de...
    b.   en service
    c.   par hasard

    d.   se sentant menacé
    e.   sur le coup

8. Find the French for:

    a.   in their turn
    b.   what had just happened
    c.   will take place
    d.   people are saying
    e.   self-defence

9. Translate the last part of the article, from: L'enquête ...   to the end.

Paper 20: S

EXERCISE 1

Read the account below, then carry out the exercises based on it. NOTE: In this, as in many scholarship exams, you are expected to take note of what is in previous questions or exercises to help you with the one you are doing.

A young man is waiting for a train. The Second World War has not long ended, and things are not yet back to normal. People do not yet fully trust each other...

Le temps qu'il faisait était sans surprise. La chaleur prêtait à tout un air de lassitude et on avait envie de s'arrêter à tout moment pour s'asseoir, se reposer. Je me trouvais dans le buffet de la gare. Il n'y avait personne. Je m'étais installé assez près du zinc pour qu'on s'occupe de moi plus facilement, j'avais l'espoir en plus d'un peu de conversation, mais en vain. Le barman, qui m'avait vu entrer dans l'établissement un peu avant midi faisait semblant de rien apercevoir, prit tout son temps et parut enfin, l'air fatigué.
    - 'jour.
    - Bonjour.
    - Qu'est-ce que vous voulez?
J'avais interrompu sa lecture et il m'en voulait, sans doute. Il était habillé en bras de chemise, et on voyait les cercles de transpiration à l'hauteur de ses aisselles. Sur ses bretelles grises, il y avait des taches sombres.
    - Une Suze.

Il me servit, presque à contrecoeur, aurait-on dit, et alla se rasseoir aussitôt derrière la cloison qui le séparait de sa clientelle. Quelqu'un appelait de plus loin.
- Marcel!
- J'arrive!

Avant de se déranger une deuxième fois, Marcel acheva de lire l'article, et ce ne fut qu'après deux ou trois minutes qu'il se leva en soupirant et se dirigea vers le fond de l'arrière-cuisine. Je ne le vis plus. Je mis ce qu'il me restait de petite monnaie sur le zinc, avalai les dernières gouttes de mon verre, et sortis sur le quai pour attendre mon train. C'était à ce moment-là que je savais où j'avais connu ce 'barman'. Il était commissaire dans la Police Allemande pendant la guerre − un collaborateur − un traître − et le voilà qui servait ses boissons dans un bar comme si rien ne s'était passé...

a) Answer these questions in English:

1. What was the weather like?
2. How many people were in the bar apart from the barman himself?
3. Where did the writer sit, and why did he choose this place?
4. What did the barman do, when the writer entered?
5. What did the writer assume the barman had been doing when he came in?
6. What shows that the barman was hot?
7. What did the barman do after serving the young man?
8. Why did the barman get up again?
9. What did the young man do before going out to wait for his train?
10. Explain as clearly as you can what it was that the young man suddenly realised, once he was outside.

11. Give the meanings of the following phrases. If you prefer, you may explain them clearly in English rather than translating them:

    a. un air de lassitude
    b. faisait semblant de...
    c. il m'en voulait, sans doute.
    d. (Il) alla se rasseoir
    e. ce ne fut qu'après deux ou trois minutes

12. Find the French expressions in the passage that mean the following:

    a. took his time
    b. almost grudgingly

c. before disturbing himself
d. what small change I had left
e. so I could be served more easily

13. Translate the last part of the passage, from "Je mis... " to the end, into English.

EXERCISE 2

1. Using the passage and what you have learnt by doing the exercises, translate the following into French.

   The cold weather gave everything an atmosphere of sadness. I found myself in the Café de la Paix. There were only three other people. One of the others was the barman. I'd seen him come in. He'd interrupted our conversation, but I wasn't angry with him.

   (Sadness: tristesse, f.)
   Note: to be angry with someone: en vouloir à quelqu'un

2. Write a few lines in French, saying what you think happened next. Don't write more than 35 words.

Paper 21: S

EXERCISE 1

Read the following passage, then attempt the exercises based on it. Answer the comprehension questions in the language of the questions.

A girl's mother is angry with her for being thoughtless.

Sophie éprouvait de la difficulté à persuader sa mère que ce n'était pas de sa faute si on ne pouvait pas rentrer avant huit heures.

— Si seulement tu avais pensé à nous, disait celle-là, on aurait été là, devant la télé, il y a au moins une heure!

— Mais maman, a répondu l'autre, l'air découragée, tu sais bien que c'est toi qui nous a dit que cela fait du bien aux personnes âgées que les jeunes mettent un peu de temps à bavarder avec elles.

— Oui, mais toi tu savais qu'on t'attendait devant la boulangerie. J'étais là depuis midi dix, il est déjà deux heures moins le quart!

— Bon, bon, a répliqué Sophie, mais il devrait y avoir un autre car?

— Pas avant huit heures dix!

— Excuse-moi, maman, mais Madame Dernoncourt voulait discuter, et puis personne ne va jamais la voir chez elle, elle est entourée de personnes qu'elle déteste, elle ne sort presque jamais à cause de tous ces escaliers, tu sais, à son âge, et l'ascenseur est toujours en panne... enfin... je la plains!

— Tu la plains! Tu la plains? Dis donc, qu'est-ce qu'on va faire jusqu'à huit heures?

Il est vrai que Sophie savait que sa maman avait bien raison, qu'elle commençait à penser à ce que son papa allait imaginer en rentrant à une maison vide, sans lumière, sans rien à manger...

Sophie n'avait plus rien à dire. Sa maman s'est tue, a pris un bouquin dans son sac à main, et s'est mise à lire. Ou, plutôt, elle a baissé les yeux vers les pages. Elle était trop en colère pour lire...

Answer these questions in English:

1. Of what did Sophie find it difficult to convince her mother?
2. What had made Sophie late?
3. Where had her mother been waiting?
4. What time is it "now"(in the passage)?
5. When will the next coach be arriving?

Répondez en français:

6. Pourquoi est-ce que Sophie plaint Madame Dernoncourt?
7. Qu'a fait la mère de Sophie, après avoir écouté sa fille?
8. Pourquoi ne lisait-elle pas vraiment?

Trouvez le français pour:

9. She was experiencing difficulty in persuading...
10. If only you'd thought of us...
11. There should be another coach.
12. She began to read.
13. She was too angry to...

EXERCISE 2

Write a letter to a friend in French, in which you relate a similar series of events. Note the following differences:

1. you were trying to persuade your father;
2. the old age pensionner you were visiting was a man;
3. you caused your father and yourself to miss the train;
4. your father was to angry to speak to you.

EXERCISE 3

Translate the part of the passage from "Si seulement... " to " ...avec elles" into good English.

EXERCISE 4

Traduisez en français:

But you knew that they were waiting for you outside the cinema! They'd been there since four-thirty. Nobody ever goes to see a film with them; I feel sorry for them!

Paper 22: S

EXERCISE 1

Lisez attentivement le passage suivant, puis répondez aux questions et faites les exercices ci-dessous:

Jérôme a ouvert lentement la porte de la chambre et en est sorti doucement, espérant ne pas réveiller sa femme. Descendant à la cuisine, il a retrouvé le chat qui s'est mis tout de suite à miauler, afin d'obliger son maître de lui donner son petit déjeuner. Mais Jérôme pensait sérieusement à autre chose. Il n'était que quatre heures du matin; un beau matin de juin, pourtant Jérôme ne voyait pas l'aube avec ses belles couleurs, l'évaporation légère de la rosée, les feuilles de ce vert vif de jeunesse qui filtraient les premiers rayons de soleil...

Un moment de terreur l'a immobilisé lorsqu'il croyait entendre le bruit, en haut, de sa femme qui se levait, mais le moment est passé, et le calme s'est aussitôt rétabli.

Il a tourné avec soin la clé dans la porte de la cuisine et en est sorti. L'air froid matinal l'a surpris, et il a aperçu non sans étonnement son haleine apparaître devant lui dans la lumière du soleil.

1. Est-ce que Jérôme habitait seul dans la maison?
2. Comment sait-on qu'il voulait quitter la maison sans être vu?
3. Pourquoi le chat a-t-il commencer tout de suite à miauler?
4. Pourquoi est-ce que son maître n'a pas nourri le chat?
5. Quel temps faisait-il, ce matin-là?
6. Pourquoi est-ce que Jérôme a été saisi d'un moment de peur?
7. Décrivez ses sentiments en sortant de la cuisine.

EXERCISE 2

A l'aide du passage que vous venez de lire, exprimez les phrases suivantes en français:

a. It was only seven o'clock in th evening.
b. A lovely September afternoon.
c. He though he saw someone.
d. The sound of her children getting up.
e. He carefully opened the car door.

EXERCISE 3

Rewrite the following sentences', completing them by translating the bracketed parts into French:

    f. (going upstairs) à la salle de bains, il (opened) la fenêtre.
    g. L'enfant (began to) crier, (with the intention of) effrayer le chien.
    h. Il espérait (not to hear) grincer les gonds de la porte du jardin.
    i. (And yet) il ne voyait pas (the rain) (which) tombait.
    j. Il a remarqué (not without surprise) qu'elle (had gone).

EXERCISE 4

Rewrite the following sentences, using pronouns to replace the underlined parts:

1. Jérôme n'a pas vu le chat.
2. Marie-Claire et Sophie sont sorties de la cuisine.
3. Son maître est monté directement dans la salle de bains.
4. Les feuilles filtraient les premiers rayons de soleil.
5. J'ai entendu Pierre qui se lavait en haut.

EXERCISE 5

Rewrite in the tenses indicated:

1. Il a ouvert soigneusement la porte.   (au présent)
2. Il croyait entendre sa femme se lever.   (au passé composé)
3. Sa femme ne remarquait pas ce qui se passait.   (au passé composé)
4. Tu me donnes la clé.   (à l'impératif)*
5. Il n'est que deux heures du matin.   (à l'imparfait)*

*—— Read 4 and 5 carefully! ——

Paper 23: S

A BIT OF A BREAK!

Translate this passage in which an employee of the newspaper Le Monde has a rather tongue-in-cheek go at the practice of searching employees who resort to shoplifting. It is in slang: note the 'vocab' as you go, and feel free to translate it loosely!

Vous, je ne sais pas, mais nous, ici, au canard(1), c'est le gros malaise. Hier soir je quitte sur le coup (2) de cinq heures et demie, je rattrape une copine dans l'escalier: Tu rentres en métro? Attends, je pars avec toi. Arrivés devant le bâtiment, rue des Italiens (3), elle baisse la tête, presse le pas (4), et elle me fait: Allez, vite! Dépêche-toi!

— Pourquoi? Qu'est-ce qu'il y a?

— Il paraît qu'ils auraient dans l'idée (5) de surveiller la sortie du personnel: contrôle des sacs à main, fouille à corps (6), enfin, tu vois...

— Pourquoi ils feraient ça?

— Tu as bien vu ce qui se passe dans les hypermarchés. Ils sont littéralement dévalisés (7) par les employées. C'est effarant (8), ce qu'elles se permettent. Piquer (9), en fin de la journée, avant de la jeter à la poubelle, un carré d'ananas, offert à la dégustation (10) de la clientelle, prendre une prune à moitié pourrie (11) au rayon des fruits et légumes. Non, mais c'est dingue (12). On en a choppé (13) une. Tu ne devineras jamais ce qu'elle a eu le culot (14) de voler: une paire de lacets!

Claude Sarraute, Le Monde, 18 mars 1988.

Vocabulaire
1. slang for newspaper; 'rag'.
2. on the dot of...
3. (the address of the newspaper offices).
4. presser le pas - to walk more quickly; to get a move on.
5. 'they've taken it into their heads to...'

6. body search.
7. 'cleaned out'

8. alarming; astounding.
9. to 'nick', 'pinch'.
10. sampling (usually tasting)

11. à moitié - half (half way in a process); pourri - rotten
12. crazy.
13. chopper - to catch someone.
14. the 'cheek', the nerve.

Paper 24: S

EXERCISE 1

Lisez attentivement le passage qui suit, puis répondez aux questions et faites les exercices.

Quand j'étais jeune, il m'arrivait assez souvent d'aller chez ma tante, qui habitait à Paris. Elle occupait un petit studio rue Clovis, dans le quartier latin, où elle menait une vie drôlement intéressante. Elle n'avait jamais assez d'argent, ne fumait que de petites cigarettes russes et portait exclusivement des vêtements de gitane.

Inutile de dire que maman la trouvait bizarre, mais elle savait que pour moi la tante Élodie représentait en quelque sorte la liberté.

En plus, ma mère profitait de mon absence pour passer quelques jours de calme avec mon père. A cette époque-là, j'avais seize ans. D'habitude, j'y passais quatre ou cinq jours, et au cours de ces visites j'ai fait la connaissance d'un monde différent et intéressant: des artistes, des poètes, des écrivains, des musiciens.

Je dirais que cela m'a ouvert les yeux.

1. Où habitait la tante de l'auteur de ce récit?
2. Comment était son appartement?
3. Pourquoi la mère de l'auteur trouvait-elle la tante bizarre?
4. Pourquoi est-ce que sa mère permettait à l'auteur de continuer à fréquenter sa tante?
5. Qu'est-ce qui se passait pendant ces visites?
6. Que pense l'auteur de cette période de sa jeunesse?

EXERCISE 2

Trouvez le français pour les phrases suivantes:

1. I quite often went...
2. She led a really interesting life.
3. She wore nothing but gipsy clothes.
4. Needless to say...
5. At that time...

EXERCISE 3

Exprimez en français:

1. I quite often stayed.
2. They led a dull life.
3. We ate nothing but vegetables .
4. Needless to say, they're rich.
5. At that time, she was eleven.

EXERCISE 4

Rewrite the following sentences with the verbs in brackets in the appropriate tenses:

1. Quand tu y arriveras, tu me (téléphoner).
2. Si je savais où envoyer la lettre, je leur (écrire) tout de suite.
3. Si je (savoir) à quel point il me détestait, je ne lui aurait jamais écrit.
4. J'espère que tu (vouloir) venir avec nous demain; ce (être) chouette.
5. Pourquoi ne (finir) -tu pas tes devoirs? Ça fait deux heures que tu (travailler).
6. Ile me (arriver) à cette époque-là d'aller voir des films policiers.

EXERCISE 5

Following on from the story in the passage, write out this further extract with what you think are appropriate words in the gaps:

Un (............), par un temps superbe de printemps, je me trouvais en (..........) chez ma tante quand un de (............) amis, un poète (............) je connaissais à peine, m'a rencontré dans la rue et m'a proposé de (............) un café avec lui (............) bistrot d'en face. J'ai accepté volontiers, et il me parlait longtemps de (..........) nouvelle collection de poèmes.   (.............) tard, en (.............) chez ma tante, je lui ai raconté tout ce qui était passé.

Paper 25: S

Dictée and Reproduction

A word or two about **Dictée**. For a long time its inclusion in exams has been questioned, since it is not representative of a 'real-life' activity. However, it is an exercise that tests very effectively a variety of language skills: you cannot succeed at it without being competent to a high standard in all sorts of **grammar,** with great emphasis on **verbs** and anything requiring **agreement.** You have to make sense of what you hear, which brings in your **listening** skills, and be able to write it down accurately and check it, which means knowing, out of the possibilities, which one is right and why.

Consider the sentence: Il mange.

Not very exciting, but is that how you write it? Could it have been: Ils mangent. ? Who was the teacher talking about when he read it out? He   or   They ?

Here are a few Dictées to get you into the right ways of thinking.   Either study them, to see what they are testing you on, or work from them in the way intended, and try to write them as they are dictated to you.

Remember, several major independent senior schools still use Dictée as a test in their scholarship French exams.

EXERCISE 1

Jean mange, il mange un oeuf. /   Jean et Michel mangent, ils mangent des oeufs. J'ai acheté un vélo. / J'ai toujours voulu / acheter un vélo. Quel vélo as-tu acheté? / Le vélo qu'elle voulait?

EXERCISE 2

Ma tante a loué une maison / au bord de la mer. / La maison qu'elle a louée est / celle de sa mère, / mais c'est le maire / qui y habite / maintenant.

EXERCISE 3

Je m'appelle Marie. / J'allais appeler ma soeur, Claudine, / pour lui parler de notre tante. / Nous l'avons vue dans la rue / mais / elle ne nous a pas reconnues. Ma soeur a les cheveux roux / comme les roues de la voiture / de papa.

EXERCISE 4

La première fois / que j'ai vu ma grand-mère / chez elle, / elle était en train
de faire / un gâteau aux fraises / pour le repas du soir. / Moi, j'adore les
gâteaux de toutes sortes. / Nous étions arrivés, / maman et moi, / quelques
minutes avant, / et ma grand-mère / ne nous a pas remarqués / entrer dans
son petit jardin. / Ma mère était bien contente / de revoir sa mère à elle, /
et de la retrouver / en pleine action / dans la cuisine. / Soudain, maman
l'a appelée.

Reproduction is the exercise where a story is read to you and you have to write it
down. Some candidates are put off by thinking that they can't use the same words
and expressions as in the reading. This is not the case. You are usually provided
with a brief outline anyway, and are expected to tell the story **as accurately as
possible,** sticking as closely as you can to the original.

Again, study the following example, or try to write it out having had it read to you.

The Long Lost Brother.

J'avais décidé de passer mes vacances à Nice, parce que j'avais besoin d'un peu de
soleil. Et puis, je n'avais pas vu mon frère depuis cinq ans, et je savais qu'il vivait
quelquepart dans la région.
Je suis arrivé à l'aéroport de Nice, où je suis monté dans un taxi jaune.
  – Hôtel le Goëland, ai-je dit.
  – Oui monsieur, a répondu le chauffeur.
Je me suis installé confortablement et j'ai pris mon journal. J'ai commencé à lire,
et j'ai vite trouvé un article qui m'intéressait. Il faisait très beau, et j'étais content
d'avoir choisi Nice pour mes vacances.
  – C'est loin?
  – Ah non, monsieur. À 2 kilomètres.
J'avais l'impression que le chauffeur me regardait dans le rétroviseur. Nous nous
sommes arrêtés, et j'allais descendre. Mais le chauffeur s'est retourné et me regardait
fixement, à travers ses lunettes de soleil.
  – Qu'est-ce qu'il y a?
  – Alors, Georges, tu ne me reconnais pas?
C'était mon frère.

Vacances à Nice –   soleil –   depuis cinq ans –   l'aéroport –   le taxi
jaune –   le Goëland –   installé confortablement –   journal –
le rétroviseur –   regarder fixement –   lunettes de soleil.

Paper 26: S

EXERCISE 1

Read the following newspaper report, then answer the questions below and do the exercises based on it.

Vosges: Un avion s'écrase contre les montagnes

Il s'est produit, le matin du 9 février, un accident du type qu'on espérait ne plus voir arriver, derrière un village perdu dans la forêt de Gérardmer dans les Vosges. Un AirVan Z390 de la Supair a pris feu sans raison apparente en s'approchant de l'aéroport de Strasbourg où il devait atterrir vers huit heures.

Après avoir décollé à Madrid une heure et demie plus tôt, les pilotes n'ont rien rapporté d'anormale pendant presque tout le vol.

Juste après 7 h 50, un membre de l'équipage a signalé au contrôle de la navigation aérienne strasbourgeois qu'il émanait de la fumée d'un des réacteurs de droite. Quelques instants plus tard, un garde forestier qui travaillait dans une clairière à 200 mètres de la R.N. 43, a vu passer l'appareil, qui volait bas "à faire peur", et d'où sortaient déjà de longues flammes jaunes. On a entendu l'explosion peu après, et, d'après les premiers constats des témoins sur scène, il n'y a aucun rescapé.

1. Where did the incident take place?
2. What is said about the cause of the fire?
3. What were the departure airport and destination of the aeroplane?
4. At which stage of its journey did the incident happen?
5. What time had it taken off?
6. What was the first indication to anyone on the ground that something had gone wrong?
7. To whom was this reported?
8. Where was the first eye-witness standing?
9. What did this person see?
10. According to first reports, how many survivors are there?

EXERCISE 2

Trouvez dans l'article le français pour:

a. an accident has happened
b. getting near to Strasbourg airport

   c. it was due to land
   d. (he) saw the aircraft going overhead
   e. (they) didn't report anything unusual

EXERCISE 3

Exprimez en français:

   f. a strange thing has happened
   g. coming up to the teacher's desk
   h. she was due to appear
   i. he heard the helicopter take off
   j. no-one saw anything bad

EXERCISE 4

Write a story in similar, rather journalese French, about a train crash. Don't be too ambitious; just see if you can use the same sort of expressions in the same way as they have been used here. Don't rush it: look carefully at the language used and see how it works.

1. Your train crash happened between Lyon (the destination) and Paris, at night.
2. Say at what point of the journey the crash happened.
3. It left the rails (no other train was invloved).
4. There were deaths and injuries, but plenty of survivors.
5. Mention the rescue services (see below).

Vocabulary:

train-driver:	le mécanicien
points:	les aiguillages
signals:	les signaux
emergency services:	le SAMU*, les sapeurs-pompiers.
injured person:	un(e) blessé(e)
dead person:	un mort
to extract:	extraire
crane:	une grue

*Service d'Aide Médicale d'Urgence   (SAMU is a whole lot easier to say, especially in an emergency!)

Paper 27: S

Les Actualités

Lisez-vous les journaux? Regardez-vous les infos (les informations) à la télé? Si vous allez réussir un concours de bourse il faut être au courant de ce qui se passe dans le monde. Pouvez-vous répondre à ces questions?

1. Comment s'appelle le Président de la République Française?
2. Comment s'appelle le train qui roule sous la Manche?
3. Qui s'est chargé de trouver une formule pour la paix au Moyen-Orient?
4. Comment s'appelle la maladie qui est née en Inde mais qui menace la santé d'autres peuples?
5. Les habitants de quelpays ont voté le 16 octobre 1994, pour dire "Oui" à l'Europe?

EXERCISE 1

Read the following article, then answer the questions which follow it.

ALERTE À LA PESTE EN INDE

On craint qu'il va y avoir une épidémie en Inde. La peste pulmonaire a tué une centaine de personnes dans la ville de Surat (dans le nord), mais il en existe des milliers d'autres qui sont soignées dans les hôpitaux. C'est la première apparition de la maladie en Inde depuis plus de trente ans, une maladie qu'on considérait vaincue.

La peste pulmonaire est transmise facilement en Inde, grâce à la présence des nombreux rongeurs dans les grandes villes. Les puces qui vivent sur les rats n'ont qu'à mordre un homme pour qu'il attrape le virus.

Une fois mordue, une personne peut aussi facilement passer la maladie à une autre en toussant ou en éternuant. Les autorités ont dû demander à l'OrganisationMondiale de la Santé de venir à leur aide: on a peur, et non sans raison, que cette maladie oubliée ne revienne dans d'autres pays du monde.

Au mois d'octobre quelques passagers débarquant d'un avion en provenance d'Inde ont été détenus à Londres, où ils ont dû subir un examen médical.

1. How many have already died from the disease?

2. What does it say about thousands of others?
3. Why has this taken everyone by surprise?
4. How is the disease carried?
5. How is to transmitted to people?
6. How is transmitted from person to person?
7. Whose help has been sought by the Indian authorities?
8. What happened in London, according to the last two lines of the report?

EXERCISE 2

Read the following report, then answer the questions below.

Le Train au Quai numéro 3, à destination de Londres...

Le train qui pourra, enfin, vous déposer de l'autre côté de la Manche, va faire ses débuts le 14 novembre. Les T.G.V. qui relieront la capitale britannique avec Paris et Bruxelles s'appeleront Eurostar.

Au mois d' octobre, on a fait un premier voyage avec des actionnaires à bord, mais pour cet événement prestigieux, sous les yeux de toute l'Europe, il y a eu des problèmes techniques et on a dû abandonner la première locomotive pour en prendre une autre.

Les compagnies de chemin de fer des trois nations (la France, la Grande-Bretagne et la Belgique) envisagent la possibilité d'un train par heure, partant des capitales de ces pays. Mais pour le présent, la circulation de ces trains reste difficile à cause des essais que l'on fait encore dans le tunnel.

1. When was the official start date of this service?
2. Which places will be linked by the new service?
3. Who was on the first, pre-launch trip?
4. Why was it a bit of a flop?
5. What is the intended frequency, once the service is underway?
6. Why is a full service being held up at the moment?

Now assemble all the new vocabulary you have learnt, found out, worked out or need to look up, from this paper.

Research, write down and learn.

Paper 28: S

Oral Exam 'Situations'

You are given the 'situation' before the oral test, with enough time to prepare it before you begin the test.

SITUATION 1.

You are talking to a French friend, who is played by the examiner, about your last holidays, when your family rented a villa. The holiday was not a total success. Use the details below to help you, and try to respond in a suitable way if the examiner asks you questions.

- prendre le train de Londres
- mal dormir
- arriver à Avignon
- prendre le petit déjeuner dans le train
- quel temps faisait-il?
- taxi
- arriver au village (qui s'appelle comment?)
- trouver la villa
- très loin de la mer
- se plaindre au propriétaire (Qu'est-ce qu'il a dit?)

SITUATION 2

You are staying with your French penfriend. He lives in a beautiful, historic town by the sea. You and he visit the town one day, at the end of which you meet up with some of his friends in a café. You tell one of his friends (played by the examiner) about your day

- discuter en prenant le petit déjeuner (...Que faire?)
- décider de visiter (quoi?)
- aller en ville (comment?)
- arriver, décider de louer des vélos
- aller voir les murailles de la Vieille Ville
- quel temps faisait-il?
- vouloir se baigner, mais...
- (ton correspondant) a faim
- décider de manger (où?)

- aller à la plage
- se baigner, prendre un bain de soleil, etc.
- Oh! Il est (quelle heure?) Rentrer à la maison

SITUATION 3

You are explaining to the parents of your friend in France what you do to earn a little extra pocket-money. The part of one of the parents will be played by the examiner, who may ask you questions at any time. Use the guide below to help you with things to say.

- faire beaucoup de choses
- ne pas beaucoup aimer faire la vaisselle
- préférer laver la voiture
- laver la voiture (de papa seulement ou des voisins aussi?)
- tondre la pelouse en été
- nettoyer les sols (de quelles pièces?)
- gagner (combien?)
- économiser? (pour acheter quoi?)
- promener le chien (de qui?)
- faire les courses (où? pour qui?)
- fatigué (?)

SITUATION 4

You are waiting to be picked up by your parents, having travelled back from France to London by train through the Channel Tunnel. Waiting with you at Waterloo Station is a French family, with whom you have struck up a conversation. You are telling the father / mother (the examiner) about your holiday in France. You went out by coach and visited several towns on your way down.

- l'Eurostar (confortable? rapide? etc.)
- partir en vacances (comment?)
- beaucoup de circulation (où?)
- visiter un des châteaux de la Loire (Chenonceaux)
- il était (comment?)

- une journée chez un autre ami à Tours
- excursion (où?)
- finalement, rencontrer correspondant (où?)
- quand?
- quel temps faisait-il?
- content d'arriver, prendre un bain etc.

Paper 29: S

Translation

EXERCICE DE TRADUCTION EN ANGLAIS (Version)

Translate the following passage into good English. Marks are awarded for style as well as accuracy. If in difficulty, make an intelligent guess, so that the parts you can do flow smoothly and logically.

Je venais d'entrer dans la librairie juste après avoir déjeuné. J'étais en ville, car je vais au boulot rue Clancy et ce n'est pas la peine de rentrer à midi. J'avais pris un casse-croûte à la brasserie d'en face, et j'avais envie de prendre le frais avant de me renfermer dans le bureau.

J'avais l'habitude en plus, au lieu de faire la sieste, de dénicher de petites boutiques des ruelles du vieux quartier dans lequelles je pouvais bouquiner, sans qu'on essaie à tout moment de me vendre quelque chose. Librairie Hulot est un des rares exemples de ce genre de magasin. Parmi les oeuvres historiques, je rencontrai par hasard un livre dont, depuis longtemps, j'avais renoncé à la découverte. C'était un récit des aventures d'une certaine... mais cela n'a aucune importance.

Car c'était en en tournant une page que je le remarquai. Il feuilletait un guide de la région dans le rayon géographique. L'air énervé et méfiant, il ne cessait guère de se rassurer en regardant autour de lui. Soudain, le livre qui l'intéressait tellement disparut dans sa poche. C'est alors que son regard rencontra le mien.

Ne sachant que faire, je restai planté devant lui, immobile et muet. Le voleur ferma son pardessus et s'en alla, non sans me jeter un dernier regard menaçant... Je me précipitai à la caisse, où la vendeuse baissa les yeux. Suivant son regard, je vis avec horreur que mes mains tremblaient .

EXERCICE DE TRADUCTION EN FRANÇAIS (Thème)

Translate the following passage into French, being careful to apply things you have learnt elsewhere.

I'd just eaten, so naturally I wanted to unearth one of those little cafés where one can have a coffee without people constantly asking questions. Instead of finding one, I came across a man selling coffee in the street, and decided to take one away and drink it in the park.

I was just opening my newspaper when I caught sight of a teenager looking at a child's mountain bike. He seemed a little nervous. I began to read the article which I had hardly started when I heard a rattling noise, and looked up and saw the boy pick up the bicycle and take it away.

Not knowing what to do, I rushed to the park keeper, who told me to call the police.

Some Vocabulary for Papers 19S to 29S

Paper 19	par hasard	by chance	un malfaiteur	a criminal
	mencer	to threaten	avoir lieu	to take place
Paper 20	prêter	to lend	le zinc	the bar
	s'occuper de	to see to/look after	faire semblant de	to pretend to
	la transp- -iration	perspiration	une aisselle	armpit
	les bretelles	braces	la cloison	partition
	soupirer	to sigh		
Paper 21	bavarder	to chat	plaindre	to pity
	un bouquin	a paperback	rater le train	to miss the train
Paper 22	miauler	to miaow	pourtant	and yet
	l'aube	the dawn	la rosée	the dew
	se rétablir	a) to re-establish oneself	avec soin	with care
			matinal (adj.)	morning
		b) to recover from an illness	l'haleine	breath
Paper 23	le malaise	discomfort	rattraper	to catch up with
	une copine (f)	friend	surveiller	to watch over, 'keep an eye on'
	un cop<u>ain</u> (m)	friend		
	le contrôle	check, control	fouiller	to search
	deviner	to guess	un carré	a square (shape)
Paper 24	un(e) gitan(e)	gipsy	utile	useful
	en quelque sorte	in a way	un écrivain	writer
	fréquenter	to go to regularly	proposer	to suggest
	un bistrot	a small restaurant	volontiers	willingly
Paper 25	louer	to rent / hire	roux	red (hair)

la roue	the wheel	le rétroviseur	rear-view mirror
à travers	through / by way of		

Note: **de** travers = askew, facing the wrong way, lopsided, etc.

Paper 26

se produire	to happen	atterrir	to land
décoller	to take off	(enlever	to take off
		=to remove, e.g. clothing)	
anormale	unusual	l'équipage	the crew
émaner	to issue, emanate	un réacteur	a jet engine
un garde forestier	a forestry worker	une clairière	a clearing
les constats	reports, statements	un témoin	a witness
un rescapé	a survivor (of an incident)		

Paper 27

les infomations, les infos, les actualités			the news
la paix	peace	le Moyen-Orient	the Middle-East
la santé	health	un peuple	a people
la peste	the plague	pulmonaire	pneumonic, pulmonary
les poumons	the lungs		
soigner	to care for	vaincu	beaten
grâce à	thanks to	un rongeur	rodent
une puce	flea	mordre	to bite
tousser	to cough	éternuer	to sneeze
en provenance de	coming from	subir	to undergo
déposer	to set down	relier	to link
un actionnaire	shareholder	envisager	to envisage
un essai	a test		

Paper 28

se plaindre	to complain	discuter	to talk
les murailles	(defensive) walls	se baigner	to go fo a swim
tondre	to mow	la tondeuse	the mower
le sol	the floor		
(le plancher is only a floorboard floor, not a ground floor)			
économiser	to save (up)		

Paper 29

le boulot	work, job	prendre le frais	to get some fresh air
renfermer	to shut back in		
dénicher	to unearth	bouquiner	to browse in a bookshop
un oeuvre	a work		to read carefully
renoncer à	to give up	feuilleter	to leaf through

méfiant	distrustful	muet	speechless
se précipiter	to rush		

naturally	naturellement	the park	les jardins publics
to catch sight of	s'apercevoir de	teenager	un ado(lescent)
a mountain bike	un vélo tout-terrain (un VTT)		
rattling noise	un claquetis	to look up	lever les yeux
to pick up	ramasser	to take away	emporter

NOTE: The vocabulary listed above is very limited, and only useful for the range of topics used in the scholarship test papers. It is hoped, in any case, that students will try to do the work without reference to the the vocabulary lists while they are working; instead they should consult them afterwards if necessary.

Paper 30: *Further Practice*

There now follows a series of completely unrelated tasks that may be used for written as well as oral practice.

1. a. Say you've forgotten your passpost.
   b. Say you think that you are going to forget your passport.
   c. Say that you never forget your passport.
   d. Ask if he / she has forgotten his / her passport.

2. a. Ask if there is a lift.
   b. Ask where the lift is.
   c. Say you don't know where the lift is.
   d. Say you don't know if there is a lift.

3. a. Ask at what time the stables open.
   b. Ask at what time the stables opened yesterday.
   c. Ask at what time the stables will close at the weekend.
   d. Ask if the stables are open on Sundays.

4. a. Say that you've been running and that you're hot.
   b. Tell him / her that he / she will get hot if he / she runs.
   c. Ask him / her why he / she is hot.
   d. Say that yesterday you found it (the weather) hot.

5. a. Say that you'd like that one there (m).
   b. Ask if you can have that one there (f).
   c. Ask if they have any others like those (m).
   d. Ask if they will have any more like those (f) next week.

6. a. Say you have already eaten the sandwiches.
   b. Say you'd already eaten the sandwiches before Jean arrived.
   c. Say that you're going to eat them.
   d. Say that you eat them sometimes, but not with cheese.

7. a. Ask how many computer game shops there are.
   b. Ask how many (of them) there were.
   c. Ask him if he thinks there will be any computer game shops.
   d. Ask her why there aren't any street lights.

8. a. Ask if the weather is good, at the moment.
   b. Ask if the weather has been good for sailing.
   c. Say you do not think that the weather will be good tomorrow.
   d. Say that the weather is better here than in Paris.

9. a. Say that, before the crowds get here, it's very peaceful.
   b. Ask if it's usually peaceful here.
   c. Ask what time the crowds will arrive.
   d. Say it got crowded last week, after lunch.

10 a. Say that you play the piano.
   b. Say that you play cricket when you're not playing the piano.
   c. Say that while Jeanne watched t.v., you played the piano.
   d. Ask if he / she will play the piano tonight?

11.a. Ask at what age one can ride a moped.
   b. Say that you can ride a moped in England at (...) years old.
   c. Ask if he / she always goes to school on the moped.
   d. Ask if one must wear a crash helmet in France.

12.a. Say that their house is very attractive.
   b. Ask how long they have lived here.
   c. Tell them that your house in England was very beautiful.
   d. Tell them that you've just moved (house) to London.

13.a. Ask if there are any one-armed bandits (slot machines).
   b. Ask him / her if he / she ever wins any money.
   c. Say that you have never won any money.
   d. Ask if you can go there tomorrow with him / her.

14.a. Say you enjoy prawns, usually.
   b. Say you enjoyed the prawns but you weren't hungry.
   c. Say you'd like to try the prawns.
   d. Ask him / her what he / she had after the prawns.

15.a. Tell him / her that you do some sport nearly every day.
   b. Tell him / her that you did some sport four times last week at school.
   c. Ask him / her how often he / she does sport at school.
   d. Ask him / her if he / she will be playing football on Saturday.

16.a. Ask his / her first name and how to spell it.
   b. Say what your surname is, then your first name, then spell them.
   c. Ask him / her what someone else's name is (m. then f.)
   d. Tell him / her what someone else's name is.

17.a. Ask which languages one can do at his / her school apart from English.
   b. Say you do (mention 2 languages) at school.
   c. Ask how many lessons a week of (mention a language) he / she does.
   d. Ask if he / she speaks any other languages.

18.a. Ask if you can watch the weather forecast.
   b. Ask what time the weather forecast is on.
   c. Say you didn't see it (the weather forecast) yesterday.
   d. Ask what time it will be on tomorrow morning.

19.a. Say that in England people eat more in the evening than at lunch.
  b. Ask if the same is true in France.
  c. Ask what there will be for lunch tomorrow.
  d. Tell him / her that you really enjoyed lunch today.

20.a. You are on the phone: ask if this is the train station.
  b. Ask if he / she knows the number for the train station.
  c. Ask what time the trains leave for Paris on Saturdays.
  d. Ask the price of a second-class return to Calais.

21.a. Ask why the windows have shutters.
  b. Explain that the windows of English houses don't have shutters.
  c. Say that there are people who clean your windows for you.
  d. Ask them at what time they will be closing the shutters this evening.

22.a. Ask if it's necessary to reserve a seat on the coach.
  b. Say that it will be necessary to phone to reserve a seat.
  c. Say that, last year, you had to reserve a seat.
  d. Ask if you will have to change coaches at Calais.

23.a. Explain that your sister won't come with you because she is unwell.
  b. Say that your brother won't be there because he's scared of heights.
  c. Ask how to get to the swimming pool.
  d. Ask if there are any diving boards.

24.a. Say your father doesn't know how to use a sewing-machine.
  b. Ask why his / her mother needs a sewing machine.
  c. Say you have a sewing machine, but no-one uses it.
  d. Ask if your dad may borrow their sewing machine.

25.a. Say that you think their car is nice.
  b. Ask what sort of car it is.
  c. Say that your car at home is different.
  d. Ask the highest speed he / she has ever been in this car.

Common Entrance *"Option C"*

This is one of the 'optional' questions which form the 'extended' exercises in the WRITING TEST part of the paper. The candidate is offered the choice of question A or question B or question C. C is different from the other two, however, since, instead of offering somewhat vague tasks (allowing candidates a range of possibilities when tackling them), it demands knowledge of *specific skills*.

Several schools require candidates to attempt option C. On the paper, candidates are warned that they should not attempt it unless they have been specifically told they should by their teacher. Here is an example:

Option A or B: Say something about the weather.

Option C: Say that it was raining yesterday but it will be fine later this evening.

There now follows some practice in Option C tasks, and how to spot what is required.

WRITING TASKS

1. Say that, when you arrived home, the dog had eaten the sausages.
   (Passé composé of verbs + être; pluperfect tense)
2. Say that it has just stopped snowing and you are about to go outside.
   (Venir de + infin ; être sur le point de + infin)
3. Say that if M. Lenoir came home early you would go to eat in a restaurant.
   (Conditional tense , following imperfect in first clause)
4. Say that, after going to bed, you felt hungry.
   (Choosing between après avoir + pp and après être + pp)
5. Say that you were hot and thirsty but not tired.
   (Avoir chaud, avoir soif, but: être fatigué).
6. Say that at the moment you are watching a rugby match on t.v.
   (être en train de + infin)
7. Say that you had all gone to bed when the noise started.
   (Pluperfect of reflexive verb)
8. Say you ate all the chocolates that you bought.
   (Agreement of pp with preceding direct object)

9. Say that when you are eighteen, you will travel a lot in France.
   (Logical future)
10. Say that the people you stayed with still phone you every holidays.
   ('with whom I stayed'; every)

Just a few examples. Option C has the advantage of being suitable for comparative testing, since each candidate will attempt the same language structures (or should do), but it is not really certain whether it will remain in the paper in its present format or not.

Appendix *Oral exam Picture Exercises*

Self-assurance and the concept of 'fluency'

Contrary to some of my pupils' beliefs, fluency does not necessarily mean speaking French like a native, nor does it mean knowing everything there is to know about the language. If it did, very few of us could claim to be fluent.

It should be understood as: having the capacity to speak without much hesitation, in a way that shows knowledge and confidence in the things one has been taught.

In the Common Entrance picture exercises, rôle play and scholarship situations, this aspect of one's competence is really put to the test. Whatever form the picture exercises take in the future, they will almost certainly continue to require the candidate to speak about a series of **events,** happening in the **past,** set against a background of **descriptive** scene-setting.

Do try to master the expressions that follow. They are arranged in a way that allows them to be learnt, not just recognized. **Learn** them and learn to string more and more of them together in an interesting and varied way.

LANGUAGE FUNCTIONS

Each element of what you say has a different function: stringing them together creates ideas which can then be linked to others:

Je suis allé (VERB OF GOING)

> au tabac (WHERE YOU WENT)

> où (LINKWORD)

> j'ai acheté un journal (WHAT YOU DID NEXT)

> puis (LINKWORD)

> (on to next idea, etc.)

On the next page are some ideas for learning the major expressions you will certainly need for this type of test.

WHERE YOU WENT

Je suis allé(e)	I went
Je suis entré(e) dans	I went in(to)
Je suis sorti(e) de	I came out (from)
Je suis monté(e)	I went up
Je suis descendu(e)	I went down

WHAT YOU DID

J'ai trouvé	I found
J'ai vu	I saw
J'ai traversé	I crossed
J'ai visité	I went round (e.g. a château)
J'ai regardé	I looked, browsed

POSITION WORDS TO LOCATE THINGS

dans	in, into	devant	in front of, outside
sur	on, on top of, onto	sous	under
le long de	along	à côté de	beside
juste à côté	just nearby	de l'autre côté de	on the other side of
juste avant	just before	un peu après	a little beyond
à droite (de)	to the right (of)	à gauche (de)	to the left (of)
dessus	on it	dessous	under it
dedans	in(side) it		

VOCABULARY

la rue	the street	la route (principale)	(main) road
le pont	the bridge	le rond-point	the roundabout
le carrefour	the crossroad	les feux	traffic lights
le poste de police	police station	le commissariat	police h.q.
la caserne	barracks	la mairie	town hall

l'hôtel de ville	town hall	le complexe sportif	sports centre
la boutique	shop	le magasin	shop
la boulangerie	bakery	la pâtisserie	pastry/cake shop
le charcuterie	delicatessen	la boucherie	butcher's shop
le café	café, bar	le restaurant	restaurant
l'église	church	les vitraux	stained-glass
la cathédrale	cathedral		windows
le cinéma	cinema	la bibliothèque	library
la poste	post-office	la gare (SNCF)	train station
la gare routière	bus station	le tabac	newsagent
le magasin de...	the ... shop	le marchand de...	the person who
le super(marché)	supermarket		sells ...
le hyper(marché)	hypermarket	l'épicerie	small supermarket
la plage	the beach	la campagne	countryside
le verger	orchard	le champ	field
un avion	aeroplane	le port	port, harbour
l'aéroport	airport	la douane	customs
le collège	school(middle)	le lycée	school (senior)
l'école	school (in general)	la cour	the playground
le court (de tennis)	(tennis) court	le terrain de foot	football pitch
le château	castle, château	les murailles	defensive walls
la tour	tower	la tourelle	turret
le ciel	the sky	le nuage	cloud
un oiseau	bird	l'escalier	staircase
un escalier	spiral staircase	une montgolfière	hot-air balloon
en colimaçon			
une auberge	country inn	un phare	lighthouse
une sation-service	filling station	l'autoroute	motorway
la vache	cow	un arbre	tree
une clôture	fence, enclosure	une barrière	gate
un portail	(town) gate	une porte cochère	gate in a wall
la rivière	river	un canot	rowing boat
un pêcheur	fisherman	un poisson	fish

The above are just a selection of words that have been useful in the picture exercises in Common Entrance over the past few years.

MAKING YOUR 'STORY' INTERESTING

Don't forget to use linkwords, and make one longer sentence out of two shorter ones.

Don't forget to **do things** at the places you 'go' to:

In a shop, you **looked**, then, perhaps, **bought** something.
       Say how much it **cost.** Was it **cheap? expensive?**
       You **went round** the château. What was it like? Give your **opinion.**

Add another bit of interest by **not** doing something:

       You looked around, **but** you didn't buy anything **because** it was expensive.

LINKWORDS

Après ça	after that	plus tard	later	puis	then
ensuite	next	un peu plus tard	a bit later		
enfin	finally				

Quand j'y suis arrivé,...   When I got there,...

GIVING YOUR OPINION

You might be asked your opinion:

C'était comment? What was it like? Comment tu l'as trouvé?
                                   What did you think of it?

Use 'trouver': Je l'ai trouvé	beau /belle	
	formidable	great
	super	really good
	extra	brilliant
	épatant	wonderful
	énorme	huge
	impressionnant	impressive
	sensass	fantastic
	chouette	brilliant

or 'être':	C'était:		
		ennuyeux	boring
		intéressant	interesting
		bruyant	noisy
		bizarre	odd, strange
		joli	pretty

ET FINALEMENT

Use what the examiner says to you to pick up on: examiners often chip in to keep the conversation going, and tend to use expressions which will prompt you to say something useful:

Qu'est-ce que tu as   **vu**?   J'ai   **vu** ...

                              trouvé?

                              pris?

                              mangé?

                              bu?

                              etc.

Be especially careful of : Qu'est-ce que tu as **fait**? , because 'fait' is not usually repeated, since the question means 'What did you do?'.

If you are not alone, change your verb forms from 'je' to 'on' or 'nous'.

Fin de la Deuxième Partie